C000178709

MY ART OF ENTERTAINING

To my father, who loved life and people,
and from whom I inherited my love
of big lively gatherings around a table
and sharing delicious meals.

FRENCH EDITION

Editorial Director: Ronite Tubiana
Editor: Clélia Ozier-Lafontaine
Design: Claude-Olivier Four and Christophe Roué

ENGLISH EDITION

Editorial Director: Kate Mascaro
Editor: Helen Adedotun
Cover Design: Audrey Sednaoui
Translation from the French: Ansley Evans
Copyediting: Wendy Sweetser
Typesetting: Claude-Olivier Four
Proofreading: Carey Jones
Production: Louisa Hanifi-Morard and Marylou Deserson
Color Separation: IGS-CP, L'Isle d'Espagnac, France
Printed in Bosnia and Herzegovina by GPS Group

Simultaneously published in French as
Mon art de recevoir: Recettes et conseils par Héloïse Brion
© Flammarion, S.A., Paris, 2022

English-language edition
© Flammarion, S.A., Paris, 2022

editions.flammarion.com

22 23 24   3 2 1

ISBN: 978-2-08-024854-1

MY ART OF ENTERTAINING

Recipes and Tips from

MISS MAGGIE'S
—— KITCHEN ——

Héloïse Brion

PHOTOGRAPHY BY

Christophe Roué

Flammarion

CONTENTS

PREFACE

À Table!

As a child, I always loved hearing those words: "Dinner time!"
I relished the prospect of a delicious meal, of course, but I
also sensed that, at the dinner table, I was about to embark
on a journey of discovery. Because, although I truly believe
that what is on our plate is of utmost importance, the table
setting—no matter how simple it is—is just as essential.
Together, they constitute a moment captured in time, an
unforgetable experience, and an invitation to share.

At my home, the table decor is always unique. It varies with
the seasons, my mood or fancy, my inspirations at the time,
the menu, and the occasion. I allow myself the freedom to
mix styles and I give my creativity free rein rather than
adhering to old, outdated conventions. After all, the most
important thing is to convey joy and warmth. I am convinced
that these moments around the table remain etched in our
memories; my sons are proof of that. They love dining by
candlelight, adding flowers and their little treasures to the
table setting, or writing up seating plans, even when it's only
the four of us.

In this book, you will discover flavorsome recipes to savor
in each season (which can be adapted according to your
tastes or the ingredients you have on hand), as well as tips
and ideas for creating attractive seasonal table settings,
planning suggestions for parties—both at home or for
summer vacation when family and friends gather together—
and a countdown to the Christmas celebrations.

So, have fun, trust your creativeness, and enjoy and share
the delight. That's what life is all about!

—Héloïse

SEVEN TIPS FOR CREATING BEAUTIFUL TABLESCAPES

TIP #1
SET THE SCENE

A simple way to create a cohesive style for your table setting is to keep certain base elements neutral (the tablecloth, glasses, a wooden or stone table, etc.) and to add color using flowers, napkins, ribbons, candles, and so on. NB: lighting is key, especially at dinner, and candlelight casts a particularly flattering glow. Place candles all around, but avoid scented candles on the table during meals.

TIP #2
DECORATE YOUR TABLE WITH FLOWERS

I often begin with flowers as inspiration for my table settings: a few pretty blooms mixed with simple elements, for example, create a light, fresh springtime tablescape. And think beyond ordinary vases: repurpose other containers like jars or buckets, fill little wooden crates with jars of flowers, or use foraged finds from your garden or woodland strolls such as flowering branches or vines of ivy. Place them down the center of your table, as this adds texture and color—and will look simply stunning. You can

then have fun adding flowers (with their stems removed) and candles here and there. If it's not peak flower season, or just to change things up a bit, make use of seasonal produce such as squash, artichokes, apples, cabbages, or turnips, in your table settings.

TIP #3
PLAY WITH DIFFERENT MATERIALS

Using a mix of contrasting materials gives tables a nice twist. For example, combine wood and silver pieces with a vintage embroidered sheet to create a rustic chic look; this laid-back yet elegant vibe is perfect for romantic dinners or springtime parties.

TIP #4
CONSIDER THE HEIGHT OF THINGS

Make sure the top of your centerpiece is low enough so that guests don't have trouble seeing one another across the table. If you have very tall candle holders, varying the height of your candles can produce a striking effect—just be careful not to place them right at eye level.

TIP #5
MIX STYLES

I love combining different styles: vintage tableware (often mismatched) paired with finds from my travels or artisanal pieces, or else a classic table setting with a bohemian piece or two. This makes for a unique and visually interesting tablescape, and it adds rhythm. Don't be afraid to try various pieces, removing them, putting them back again, and changing their position if it isn't working—that's part of the fun of creating an original table setting. Follow your instincts and have faith in your creative flair!

TIP #6
BREAK SOME RULES

According to certain rules of etiquette in France, champagne glasses don't belong on the dining table, but I find champagne dinners rather joyful. In a classic table setting, glasses are placed above the plates and ordered from tallest to shortest, from left to right: the tallest glass, usually for water, goes on the left, then comes a smaller glass for red wine, and so on. However, I prefer to place a bigger glass for wine to the left and a smaller one for water to the right of it. I find this more aesthetically pleasing. When it comes to napkins, though, I always make a point of using cloth napkins, even for picnics!

TIP #7
IT'S ALL ABOUT THE DETAILS

For a final, personalized touch, I usually add a little detail or gift to each place setting. This could be a rosemary sprig in flower from the garden, an inspirational quote on pretty paper, a small jar of a homemade spice blend, a lovely ribbon tied around the napkin—the possibilities are endless!

TIPS FOR HOSTING A PARTY

- Ask each of your guests to bring a dish, such as a salad, quiche, dessert, or cheese.
- Make sure you have plenty of trays, as this makes it so much easier to set up a buffet or a table in the garden.
- Create a bar area so your guests can serve themselves. Make a variety of drinks in pitchers or drink dispensers, such as water infused with cut fruits or fresh herbs; homemade lemonade; watermelon and mint juice; or cocktails.
- Set up speakers and prepare a playlist: plan on two hours of music during dinner (jazz, classical), followed by increasingly danceable tunes!
- Place candles, string lights, and lanterns everywhere: on tables and buffets, on steps, hanging from trees, etc.

- Weather permitting, get out some outdoor games for guests to play (*pétanque*; croquet; Mölkky, the Finnish throwing game; cornhole, the beanbag toss game; etc.).
- Be sure to have lemongrass on hand to fend off mosquitos, or else bouquets of fresh herbs that repel them, such as mint, sage, basil, lavender, and lemon balm.
- And if possible, have a fire pit in the garden, a guitar or two, and plenty of blankets to end the evening singing under the stars.
- My most important piece of advice, no matter the season, is to be sure to schedule a moment just for you before your guests arrive. It's essential to take a little time to relax: take a bath, apply a facial mask, have a drink with your partner. Now everything is ready, it's time to enjoy your family and friends!

CREATING THE PERFECT CHEESEBOARD

A cheeseboard with a mix of dried and fresh fruits, nuts,
and other tasty nibbles sets the tone for a warm, convivial gathering.
It's quick and easy to assemble, and is always a hit with guests.
Cheeseboards can be prepared throughout the year
and the composition varied according to what's in season
or your favorite cheeses and pairings. You can purchase
all the components or prepare a few simple extra dishes
yourself for a more personal touch. Here are four homemade recipes
to accompany your cheeseboard (see photo pp. 14–15).

SPICED PUMPKIN SEEDS

The next time you make pumpkin or squash soup, save the seeds, rinse them well, and dry them. Preheat the oven to 400°F (200°C/Gas Mark 6). Spread the seeds over a baking sheet lined with parchment paper, drizzle over a little olive oil, and sprinkle with paprika and nutmeg. Toss to coat the seeds well, then bake for about 20 minutes, until they are golden, stirring halfway through the cooking time. As soon as you remove them from the oven, sprinkle the seeds with fleur de sel and pepper. Feel free to experiment with different flavorings: thyme and lemon zest is a tasty combination, and cinnamon works well, too.

POACHED PEARS

Poached pears are so delicious with cheese! You can poach them with vanilla or cardamom, or in spiced wine as in this recipe. Place a scant 1 cup (240 ml) water, ½ cup (120 ml) red wine, 1 tsp quatre-épices spice mix, 3 star anise pods, and 3 tbsp brown sugar in a saucepan. Bring to a boil, stirring until the sugar dissolves, then let boil for 2 minutes. Immerse 2 or 3 whole peeled pears in the syrup and let simmer over low heat for 20 minutes, turning them over occasionally. Let the pears cool in the syrup, turning them often. Drain, slice thinly, removing the cores, and place in a small bowl.

CANDIED PECANS

These pecans are perfect for nibbling, serving with tea, or crumbling over ice cream—and for cheeseboards like this one! Place 1 large handful pecans in a small skillet with 2 tbsp brown sugar, the juice of 1 clementine (or ½ orange), 1–2 tbsp water, and a small pinch of ground cinnamon. Bring to a simmer and cook until the sugar dissolves. Stir until the pecans are well coated, then turn them out of the skillet onto a sheet of parchment paper, and separate using a fork. Let cool.

HOMEMADE BREADSTICK TWISTS

Here's another recipe you can adapt according to the season or what you fancy at the time. Roll 1 quantity pizza dough (see pp. 38–39) into a rectangle measuring about 10 × 12½ in. (25 × 32 cm). For the breadsticks in the photo, mix the following together in a bowl: 1 tbsp dried or fresh thyme, 1 tbsp dried oregano, 1 tbsp dried sage, the finely grated zest of 1 lemon (preferably organic), pepper, a scant ½ cup (1½ oz./40 g) grated Parmesan, 1 tbsp halved capers, and 1 tsp cumin seeds. In another bowl, combine 4–5 tbsp extra-virgin olive oil, 2 finely chopped garlic cloves, and a little fleur de sel. Preheat the oven to 400°F (200°C/Gas Mark 6) and line a baking sheet with parchment paper. Brush the pizza dough with some of the oil mixture and spread the seasoning mixture over the left half of the dough. Fold the right side of the dough over the left and press down with your fingertips to seal. Cut the dough in half crosswise, then make cuts every ¾ in. (2 cm) lengthwise to obtain about a dozen or so strips. Pick up one strip at a time, twist it, and place on the prepared baking sheet. Brush with the oil mixture and bake for 7–8 minutes, then turn each breadstick over, brush again with the oil, return to the oven for an additional 6 minutes, and bake until golden brown. As soon as you remove the breadsticks from the oven, brush them once more with the oil mixture and sprinkle with grated Parmesan. They are delicious! You can also make the breadsticks using homemade pesto, sundried tomatoes, tapenade—just have fun experimenting!

SHOPPING

Here's something I find incredibly helpful and that I do throughout the year. Before I go shopping, I take out my notepad and jot down everything I need by grouping together the various items in different categories on the sheet of paper: all the fruits and vegetables together; all the dairy products (cheeses, yogurt, butter, milk, eggs) together; all the meats and fish together; all the drinks together; and all the less exciting, but nevertheless important, items (toilet paper, sponges, trash bags, etc.). On shopping day—whether it's at the farmers' market or supermarket—this not only saves time, but it helps ensure you don't forget anything. And another thing—I also like to have a pen on me, to cross items off the list as I go and to circle anything I haven't been able to find so it stands out. This may seem rather pedantic, but even my husband, Christophe—who once looked at me strangely for doing this—has realized how effective my method is and now uses it himself. To take it one step further, visualize your farmers' market or supermarket as you make your shopping list and write down the items in order according to the aisles or stands. You will quickly discover this is a huge time saver.

It can be tricky to work out how much food you'll need to feed a crowd. Here's a table of approximate amounts to allow per person:

FOODS	PER PERSON
Crudités	About 3 oz. (90 g)
Vegetables	5–9 oz. (150–250 g)
Pasta (dried)	3½–5 oz. (100–150 g)
Meat and fish	About 5 oz. (150 g) for adults or 2½–2¾ oz. (75–80 g) for children
Bread	1–2 slices per meal, plus more if you're serving cheese

Market List

aubergines x 6
tomates 2 Kg.
courgettes 2 Kg.
abricots -20
pêches -20
figues -10

Yaourts
beurre doux
crème fraîche
oeufs
fromages

PQ
éponges
liquide vaisselle
Farine
chocolat

pain ++
brioche

sardines x30

presse

poulet x2
saucisses x20
Jambon

MISS MAGGIE'S
KITCHEN

SPRING

SPRING IS IN THE AIR!

The sound of birdsong is everywhere and once more nature turns a vibrant green. This gentle season brings with it a feeling of lightness; it is a time of rebirth in nature, when its palette of joyful, vivid hues awakens after months of hibernation.

The first sunny days of spring offer the perfect opportunity to gather family and friends together outdoors around a big table. The temperature is ideal and mosquitos aren't a nuisance yet. It's a wonderful season to spend time together in the open air, so get out the deckchairs and set up a garden table.

Keep in mind, however, that the weather may be unpredictable in early spring and can change at a moment's notice, so it's always a good idea to have a plan B up your sleeve, to move the party indoors when the heavens open—a movie or board games with hot chocolate and marshmallows, for example.

I'm a fan of serving large, family-style dishes, and I love mixing multiple generations around the table. And there's nothing like seeing your guests joyfully passing dishes around and serving each other. It's a great way for guests to get to know one another and forge bonds.

FLOWERS
Peonies, tulips, buttercups, anemones, lilacs, camellias, bellflowers, daffodils, poppies, sweet pea flowers.

TABLE DECOR
Use fresh flowers to decorate napkin rings or carafes. Choose white to honor the green shades of spring, and fresh seasonal produce in celebration of this season of rebirth.

PLACE CARD AND GIFT IDEAS
Small pots and seeds for planting; personalized vintage tea towels; homemade fresh flower wreaths; DIY place cards made with self-hardening clay.

PARTY IDEAS
When the weather turns warm, organize a buffet in your garden for lunch. In the evening, start with drinks in the garden (blankets and a fire pit are advised), before continuing the festivities inside. Organize a picnic in the great outdoors with pretty vintage picnic baskets.

MAKE FLOWERS THE STARS OF YOUR TABLE SETTINGS

Cover the table with a tablecloth (either plain or a gingham print) or, if you have an attractive wooden table, leave it uncovered. Scatter the table with ivy (often found climbing up tree trunks) and flowers with their stems cut off. Alternatively, decorate the table with flowers in painted jars and candles, or hang a garland above the table. You could also hang pretty lanterns from tree branches—experiment by placing them at different heights to create rhythm. Above all, trust your creativity. I promise you that your guests will be delighted!

Some other ideas...

Instead of displaying cut fresh flowers, buy potted flowering plants and herbs from a garden center. Hide the pots with fabric (pretty tea towels, napkins, etc.) and use them to create a centerpiece.

The day after your gathering, you can plant them in your garden or place the pots on your balcony or windowsill. That way, you can enjoy them until the end of the summer.

When serving cocktails or starters, you can incorporate seasonal produce into your table decoration. It not only looks attractive but is also perfect for nibbling. Place small bowls of sauces or different types of hummus here and there on the table for dipping.

Invent a homemade cocktail and give it a name. If it's a hit, it will stand out in your guests' memories and become a house classic.

DON'T FORGET THE MUSIC!

Music is key and helps create the atmosphere of the day or evening. You'll need speakers and playlists for the meal, and for dancing afterwards!

GRAPEFRUIT AND ROSEMARY REFRESHERS

Serves 2

ACTIVE TIME
15 minutes

INFUSING TIME
15 minutes

COOKING TIME
15 minutes

INGREDIENTS
½ cup (120 ml) water
½ cup (4 oz./120 g) packed brown sugar,
    plus extra for sprinkling
4 sprigs fresh rosemary, divided
¼ grapefruit, preferably organic,
    sliced crosswise
Ice cubes
Juice of 1 grapefruit
Citrus-flavored or plain sparkling water

1. To make a rosemary-infused syrup, heat the water and brown sugar with 2 sprigs of rosemary in a saucepan over low heat, stirring until the sugar dissolves. Let simmer for 2 minutes, then remove from the heat and let infuse until cool. Remove the rosemary and discard it.
2. Place the grapefruit slices in a hot skillet and sprinkle a little brown sugar over them. Cook over medium heat for about 5 minutes, or until caramelized, turning them once. Remove the slices from the skillet and let cool.
3. To assemble the drinks, place several ice cubes in two glasses, then add 2 tablespoons rosemary-infused syrup to each. Divide the grapefruit juice between them and top up with a little sparkling water. Stir to blend.
4. Garnish each refresher with a rosemary sprig and 2–3 caramelized grapefruit slices. Serve very cold.

KITCHEN NOTES: To turn these refreshers into cocktails, add 3½ tbsp (50 ml) vodka to each glass before adding the syrup.
For parties, make up a large quantity in a pitcher.

EGG SALAD

Serves 4

ACTIVE TIME
15 minutes

INGREDIENTS
8 hard-boiled eggs
3 tbsp mayonnaise
1–2 tbsp wholegrain mustard
½ red onion, finely chopped
2 tbsp capers, plus extra to garnish
1 lemon, preferably organic
2 tbsp finely chopped flat-leaf parsley
1 tbsp snipped chives, plus extra to garnish
Fleur de sel
Freshly ground pepper
About 10 radishes, thinly sliced

1. Peel and chop the eggs, then place them in a bowl.
2. In a small bowl, combine the mayonnaise, mustard, red onion, and capers.
3. Finely grate the zest of the lemon and juice half of it. Stir the zest and juice into the mayonnaise mixture, followed by the parsley and chives. Season with fleur de sel and pepper.
4. Stir the chopped eggs into the mayonnaise. Add the radishes, reserving a few slices for garnish. Cover and chill.
5. Serve chilled, sprinkled with extra capers, chives, and the reserved radish slices.

KITCHEN NOTES: For a picnic, you can spread the egg salad between slices of bread to make delicious sandwiches. Or for a buffet, serve it on small pieces of toast, garnished with herb flowers or other edible flowers of your choice. Your guests will love them!

PARMESAN AND GARLIC LOAF

Serves 8

ACTIVE TIME
15 minutes

COOKING TIME
40–45 minutes

INGREDIENTS
Butter and flour for the pan
2¾ tbsp (40 ml) whole milk
Juice of ½ lemon
1 stick (4 oz./115 g) unsalted
  butter, diced
¼ cup (60 ml) neutral
  vegetable oil
  (such as canola)
3 cloves garlic, finely
  chopped

2¼ cups (10 oz./280 g)
  all-purpose flour
Scant 1 tbsp (11 g) baking
  powder
1 large pinch baking soda
Leaves of a few sprigs fresh
  thyme
1 large pinch fleur de sel
A few grinds of pepper
1⅓ cups (4½ oz./130 g)
  grated Parmesan, divided
2 eggs

1. Preheat the oven to 350°F (180°C/Gas Mark 4). Grease a standard loaf pan with butter and dust it with flour.
2. Pour the milk and lemon juice into a bowl and let sit for 5–10 minutes.
3. Meanwhile, warm the butter, oil, and garlic in a skillet over low heat, until the butter melts. Stir, then remove from the heat.
4. Place the flour, baking powder, baking soda, thyme leaves, fleur de sel, and pepper in a mixing bowl. Stir to combine.
5. Stir in 1 cup (3½ oz./100 g) of the Parmesan, then mix in the eggs one at a time. Add the milk-lemon juice mixture, followed by the butter-garlic mixture. Stir until everything is just combined.
6. Pour the batter into the loaf pan and sprinkle over the remaining Parmesan. Bake for 40–45 minutes, or until the tip of a knife pushed into the center comes out clean.
7. Let the loaf cool in the pan for 5 minutes, then turn it out onto a rack. Serve warm or at room temperature.

KITCHEN NOTES: You can replace the milk and lemon juice with ¼ cup (60 ml) buttermilk. This loaf is perfect for cocktail hour. For a large gathering, cut the slices into halves or quarters. It is delicious eaten on its own, with hummus, or served with a salad.

ROASTED RADISH SALAD

Serves 3–4, as a starter or side dish

ACTIVE TIME
15 minutes

COOKING TIME
30 minutes

INGREDIENTS
9 oz. (250 g) assorted radishes
3 tbsp (1¾ oz./50 g) unsalted butter
5 whole anchovies packed in oil, drained,
  bones and tails removed
Juice of ½ lemon
5 oz. (150 g) smoked bacon,
  cut into ¼-in. (6-cm) lardons (optional)
Freshly ground pepper
A few chives, snipped
Chive blossoms, to garnish

1. Preheat the oven to 375°F (190°C/Gas Mark 5).
2. Wash the radishes, remove the tops, and cut them in half lengthwise.
    Line a baking sheet with parchment paper and place the radishes on it.
3. Melt the butter in a saucepan over low heat.
4. Meanwhile, mash the anchovies in a bowl with the lemon juice.
5. Let the butter cool for 2 minutes, then stir it into the anchovies to make a sauce.
6. Pour half the sauce over the radishes and toss to combine. Roast in the oven
    for 20 minutes.
7. Meanwhile, brown the lardons, if using, in an ungreased skillet.
    Drain on paper towels and set aside.
8. Transfer the radishes to a serving plate and mix in the lardons. Season with
    pepper, sprinkle with the snipped chives, and garnish with chive blossoms.
9. Serve with the remaining anchovy sauce.

KITCHEN NOTES: Make sure you have plenty of good bread as this sauce is addictive.

PIZZA DOUGH

Makes 1 large
or 2 medium pizzas

ACTIVE TIME
10 minutes

RESTING TIME
10 minutes

RISING TIME
40 minutes

INGREDIENTS
1 cup (250 ml) lukewarm
water

2½ tsp (8 g) instant yeast
1 tbsp brown sugar
2½ cups (10½ oz./300 g) all-
purpose flour
1–2 large pinches fleur de sel
Extra-virgin olive oil

1. Combine the water, yeast, and brown sugar in a bowl. Stir to dissolve the yeast and sugar and let rest for 10 minutes.
2. Place the flour and fleur de sel in a large bowl, then pour in the yeast mixture. Stir with a wooden spoon to make a dough (it will be sticky), add a drizzle of olive oil, and stir to incorporate the oil. Cover the bowl with a clean kitchen towel and let the dough rise in a warm place for at least 40 minutes, or until doubled or even tripled in size.
3. Turn the dough out onto a lightly floured surface and knead for a few minutes to deflate it. Dust with a little extra flour as needed, to prevent it from sticking to your fingers.
4. Divide the dough in half for two pizzas, or into smaller pieces for individual ones. Stretch into the desired shape on parchment paper. Leftover dough can be stored for up to 24 hours in the refrigerator in an airtight container or covered in plastic wrap.

BRUSSELS SPROUT AND PANCETTA PIZZA

Serves 4–5

ACTIVE TIME
15 minutes, plus making the pizza dough

COOKING TIME
35–40 minutes

INGREDIENTS
1 lb. (500 g) Brussels sprouts
Extra-virgin olive oil
2 shallots, thinly sliced
2 pinches fleur de sel
3½ oz. (100 g) pancetta, thinly sliced

1 cup (3½ oz./100 g) grated Parmesan
1 quantity pizza dough (see recipe above)
Freshly ground pepper

1. Preheat the oven to 375°F (190°C/Gas Mark 5). Wash the Brussels sprouts. Thinly slice half of them and halve or quarter the rest, depending on their size.
2. Heat a little olive oil in a skillet, add the Brussels sprouts, shallots, and fleur de sel, and cook over medium heat for 4–5 minutes, until the sprouts have softened. Remove from the heat, then add the pancetta. Stir in the Parmesan. Taste and add pepper and more fleur de sel as needed.
3. Roll or stretch the pizza dough over a sheet of parchment paper and slide it onto a baking sheet. Spread the Brussels sprout mixture over the dough, leaving a ¾–1½-in. (2–4-cm) border all around. Bake for 20–25 minutes, until the crust is golden brown. Serve immediately.

ORECCHIETTE WITH HAZELNUTS AND SAGE

Serves 4

ACTIVE TIME
10 minutes

INFUSING TIME
15–20 minutes

COOKING TIME
10 minutes

INGREDIENTS
3 tbsp (1¾ oz./50 g) unsalted butter
About 10 sage leaves
10½ oz. (300 g) orecchiette
⅓ cup (2 oz./60 g) toasted hazelnuts, roughly chopped
Parmesan or Pecorino, freshly grated
Fleur de sel
Salt and freshly ground pepper

1. Heat the butter with the sage leaves in a saucepan over low heat, until the butter melts. Let infuse over very low heat for 15–20 minutes.
2. Cook the orecchiette in a large pan of boiling salted water for about 10 minutes, or for 1 or 2 minutes less than the time indicated on the package.
3. Drain the pasta and toss it with the melted butter and sage leaves to coat.
4. Transfer the pasta to a serving bowl. Sprinkle over the hazelnuts and grate the cheese over the top according to personal taste. Season with pepper and serve immediately.

KITCHEN NOTES: You can swap out the hazelnuts for other nuts of your choice: pecans, cashews, almonds, or a mix of different nuts.

STUFFED BAKED POTATOES, TWO WAYS

Serves 6

ACTIVE TIME
10 minutes

COOKING TIME
45–55 minutes

INGREDIENTS
For the potatoes
6 large potatoes
2 tbsp (1 oz./30 g) unsalted
   butter, melted
Fleur de sel

For the filling
¾ cup (6 oz./170 g) sour
   cream
Grated cheese of your
   choice
Smoked bacon bits
Fresh chives, snipped
Fleur de sel
Freshly ground pepper
2 slices smoked trout
¼ red onion, finely chopped
2 tbsp capers
Finely grated zest
   of 1 lemon, preferably
   organic
Fresh cilantro, finely
   chopped

1. Preheat the oven to 425°F (220°C/Gas Mark 7).
2. Scrub the potatoes under cold running water. Pierce them several times all over using a fork.
3. Place the potatoes on a baking sheet (or in individual baking dishes or ramekins) and bake for 25 minutes. Brush them with the melted butter, sprinkle with fleur de sel, and place back in the oven. Continue to bake for an additional 20–30 minutes, depending on the size of the potatoes, until tender.
4. Remove the potatoes from the oven and slice them open down the middle, cutting them three-quarters of the way through.
5. Place 2 tablespoons of sour cream in the center of each potato and top with one of the following combinations:
   - Grated cheese, bacon bits, snipped chives, fleur de sel, and pepper.
   - A piece of smoked trout, chopped red onion, capers, lemon zest, fleur de sel, chopped cilantro, and pepper.
6. Serve immediately.

KITCHEN NOTES: Feel free to improvise with other filling combinations. At large gatherings or cookouts, you can set up a fillings bar, so that guests can serve themselves and create their own combinations, according to their personal taste.

PASTA AL LIMONE, MY WAY

Serves 4–5

ACTIVE TIME
15 minutes

COOKING TIME
20–30 minutes

INGREDIENTS
3 tbsp (1¾ oz./50 g) unsalted butter
Finely grated zest and juice of 3 lemons,
    preferably organic
Generous ½ cup (2 oz./60 g) grated
    Parmesan, plus extra for serving
4–5 sprigs fresh thyme
Scant ½ cup (2 oz./60 g) pine nuts
1 lb. (500 g) dried tagliatelle
8 oz. (225 g) burrata, cut into pieces
White truffle oil (optional)
A few arugula leaves (optional)
Salt and freshly ground pepper

1. Gently melt the butter over low heat in a skillet large enough to hold the pasta when cooked. Add the lemon zest and juice, and let cook for 2–3 minutes.
2. Stir in the Parmesan and the leaves of the thyme sprigs, then remove from the heat before the mixture browns.
3. Toast the pine nuts in an ungreased skillet and set aside.
4. Cook the tagliatelle in a large pan of boiling salted water for 2 minutes less than the time indicated on the package. Drain, reserving ½ cup (125 ml) of the cooking water.
5. Place the skillet with the lemon-Parmesan mixture back on the heat, with the burner turned to its lowest setting. Add the hot pasta and half the reserved cooking water. Toss to mix, adding more of the cooking water if the pasta looks dry.
6. Tip into a serving dish and scatter over the pine nuts and burrata pieces.
7. Drizzle with white truffle oil, if using, and add a few arugula leaves, if you wish. Season with salt and pepper, and serve immediately.

GÂTEAU AU CHOCOLAT

This chocolate cake is super indulgent. It takes me back to my childhood, with its gooey texture that sticks to your teeth!

Serves 8–10

ACTIVE TIME
10 minutes

COOKING TIME
17 minutes

INGREDIENTS

1 stick plus 2 tbsp (5 oz./150 g) unsalted butter, diced, plus extra for the pan

14 oz. (400 g) dark baking chocolate, chopped

5 eggs

1 cup minus 1 tbsp (6 oz./180 g) superfine sugar

¾ cup plus 2 tbsp (3½ oz./100 g) all-purpose flour, plus extra for the pan

Fleur de sel

1. Preheat the oven to 350°F (180°C/Gas Mark 4). Grease a 9-in. (23-cm) springform pan with butter, dust it with flour, and line the bottom with a disk of parchment paper (this will make it easier to unmold the cake).

2. Melt the butter and chocolate together in a saucepan over very low heat, stirring until smooth.

3. Whisk the eggs, sugar, and flour together in a mixing bowl until smooth. Pour in the melted chocolate and butter, and mix well.

4. Pour the batter into the prepared pan and sprinkle with fleur de sel. Bake for 17 minutes, until the top is dry and set but the center is still moist. Let cool before unmolding the cake and serving.

KITCHEN NOTES: You can also add pecans, chopped caramelized hazelnuts, or a pinch of cinnamon or cardamom to the batter.

ICED ORANGE AND PISTACHIO COOKIES

Makes about 30 small cookies

ACTIVE TIME
15 minutes

CHILLING TIME
20 minutes

COOKING TIME
15 minutes

INGREDIENTS
1 stick plus 2 tbsp (5 oz./150 g) unsalted butter
¾ cup (5 oz./150 g) demerara sugar, divided
Finely grated zest and juice of 2 blood oranges, preferably organic
1 egg, separated
2 cups (9 oz./250 g) all-purpose flour
2 pinches salt
Scant ½ cup (1¾ oz./50 g) shelled roasted pistachios, finely chopped
¾ cup (3½ oz./100 g) confectioners' sugar, plus extra if needed
Fleur de sel

1. Melt the butter in a saucepan over low heat. Pour it into a mixing bowl and stir in a scant ⅔ cup (4¼ oz./120 g) of the demerara sugar. Add the orange zest, reserving a little for decoration, and the juice of 1 orange. Add the egg yolk, followed by the flour, salt, and pistachios, and combine to make a dough.
2. Shape the dough into a ball, cut it in half, and roll each half into a log measuring 2–2½ in. (5–6 cm) in diameter. Cover with plastic wrap and chill for about 20 minutes.
3. Preheat the oven to 350°F (180°C/Gas Mark 4). Line 1 large or 2 medium baking sheets with parchment paper.
4. Unwrap the dough and brush each log with the egg white. Sprinkle over the remaining demerara sugar. Cut the logs into ¼-in. (5-mm) slices and place them flat on the baking sheet(s). Bake for 12–15 minutes until golden. Let cool.
5. To prepare the icing, whisk the juice from the second orange into the confectioners' sugar, 1 tablespoon at a time, until smooth. Add a little more juice or sugar to adjust the consistency, as desired.
6. When the cookies have cooled to room temperature, spoon a little icing over them, covering them partially or completely. Sprinkle over the remaining orange zest and a few fleur de sel crystals. Let the icing set, then serve the cookies with a good cup of tea!

AFFOGATO

As soon as the first sunny days appear, we like to invite our friends over for a big lunch in the garden. It's the perfect occasion for an affogato bar! All you need is a variety of ice cream flavors (vanilla, caramel, hazelnut, coffee, and chocolate are popular choices); toppings such as assorted nuts, pralines, shredded coconut, chocolate chips, chocolate-coated coffee beans, spices, caramel sauce, and Baileys Irish Cream; and very good coffee (don't forget the decaf, too). Arrange everything on a side table or on a large tray, then let your guests help themselves and create their own winning combinations. For children, you can swap out the espresso for melted chocolate. This version of the recipe—which I particularly enjoy—serves one, but the quantities can easily be increased to suit the number of guests.

Makes 1 affogato

ACTIVE TIME
10 minutes

COOKING TIME
5 minutes

INGREDIENTS
1¼ cups (5 oz./150 g) shelled roasted
   pistachios
2 tbsp sugar
1 scoop vanilla ice cream
1 pinch ground cinnamon
1 pinch ground cardamom
1 shot hot espresso

1. Place the pistachios and sugar in a skillet over low heat.
2. Stirring continuously, cook gently until the sugar dissolves and the pistachios are completely coated. Tip out onto a sheet of parchment paper and leave to cool.
3. Just before serving, place the scoop of ice cream into a glass and sprinkle with the cinnamon and cardamom. Pour the hot espresso over the ice cream.
4. Roughly chop a few candied pistachios and sprinkle over the top. Serve immediately.

KITCHEN NOTES: The leftover candied pistachios make a delicious snack, or can be stored in an airtight container at room temperature for your next affogato.

SUMMER

SUMMER VACATION AND GARDEN PARTIES

What a joy it is to get together with family and friends during summer vacation! I have such wonderful memories of my childhood, when there would be about twenty of us staying—and often thirty around the lunch or dinner table. As you can no doubt tell, I love regional, market-fresh produce, cooking, and large gatherings. Of course, these moments with my family are precious, but—let's be honest—they can also easily turn into a nightmare. If you're the only one overseeing meals and looking after guests, these occasions will quickly lose the fun factor and you'll need a second vacation by the end of the summer. I'd like to help you truly enjoy these moments without experiencing any stress, by sharing a few humble suggestions with you. Many of these tips will come in handy throughout the year.

FLOWERS
Hydrangeas, gladiolas, zinnias, dahlias, lavender, yarrow, sunflowers, cosmos, daisies.

TABLE DECOR
Repurpose vintage pillowcases into small tablecloths or placemats. Decorate with seasonal fruits. Line vases with lemon slices. Add touches of wood, linen, shells, and/or hand-painted glasses.

PLACE CARD AND GIFT IDEAS
Sparklers to kick off the festivities; sachets filled with lavender from the garden; flat peaches tied with pretty ribbons; herb bouquets; jars of homemade jam.

PARTY IDEAS
Fill large pitchers or drink dispensers with fruit- or herb-infused water. Set up a self-service bar. Line the dance floor with outdoor string lights and bales of hay. Ask musician friends to bring their instruments. Place lots of candles on the tables, along with baskets or bowls filled with fresh fruit. As a surprise, treat your guests to a tango or salsa lesson.

MAKE A WEEKLY MEAL PLAN

It feels good not to have to think too hard when you're on vacation, so give your brain a rest. Write down the week's meals (lunches and dinners) on a piece of paper and hang it up in the kitchen where everyone can see it. That way, you won't have to hear the question "What's for dinner?" incessantly, and if you're out for a walk, or immersed in a good book or hot bath, someone else can make the meal you've planned. As a double bonus, a weekly meal plan helps reduce food waste. Think to include a buffet-style "leftovers" meal, where everyone serves themselves. Not only does less food end up in the trash, but it also gives you more time to do something else or simply to relax. This is a great tradition for every Sunday evening of the year!

Other tips

I always keep two packages of dried pasta in the pantry, in case I'm feeling particularly lazy or need to improvise a meal for friends who've dropped by unannounced. That way I can continue to relax in my deckchair while I come up with a sauce using the vegetables I have on hand.

MAKE A SHOPPING LIST

See page 18 for my personal method. During the summer vacation, this method allows you to divide the list up easily among the family members or friends who are with you at the market: in my case, Jule takes care of the fruit and vegetable stand, Paloma visits the cheesemonger, and Marco heads to the fishmonger. Before you know it, all that'll be left to pick up is the bread, a newspaper, and some flowers, which means you can leisurely sip a cool drink under the plane trees, on the terrace of a local café, as you wait for the others. Not bad, right?

ORGANIZE TEAMS AND ROLES

The house in which I spent most of my vacations when I was growing up is tucked away in the mountains of the Pyrénées-Orientales region, in the south of France. For thirty-five years, there was no electricity: we had to cut and burn wood for hot water, so there was no dishwasher. But even with twenty or thirty guests (imagine all the dishes!), this wasn't a problem, because we worked in teams: one team set and cleared the table, another helped prepare the meal, and another washed the dishes (one person washed, one rinsed, and the others dried the dishes and put them away), and these tasks were always carried out to the sound of music, singing, and laughter. Today, my friends and cousins all have happy memories of these special times. If you have younger children, you can make mixed-age teams—this creates wonderful bonds. Depending on the length of your stay, you can rotate teams and roles as you wish, noting them on the meal plan hanging in the kitchen.

LET GUESTS PARTICIPATE AND GO WITH THE FLOW

We all want our guests to relax, of course, but just because we're hosting doesn't mean we have to prepare the meals by ourselves. At least one guest, if not all, will likely ask at some point if there's anything they can make, bring, or help with. Don't send them away with a cocktail—accept their offer. Ask one friend to take charge of the aperitif and another to man the grill. Or invite your friends to take over at the stove and share their specialties with you. From time to time, it feels good to be served in your own house, and friends are often delighted to participate.

RECIPES

With a few exceptions (such as birthday parties, weddings, etc.), you should not embark on complicated dishes that take all day to prepare.

· Choose recipes that are quick to make, can be popped into the oven and left to cook, or can be prepared in advance and reheated. For example, soups, lasagnas, roast chicken, and tians.

· Opt for recipes you can serve in large dishes, either family style or as part of a buffet. Guests will naturally serve those sitting next to them and the children, and this is easier and more convivial than serving one plate at a time.

· It's often easier to make two different cakes rather than one big one. This not only gives guests two choices, but it is also a safer bet in case the oven is too small for a large cake pan.

· When making a tart, double or triple the quantity of dough and store what's left in the refrigerator (or freezer), covered in plastic wrap, for another day. That's one less step to worry about the next time!

· Prepare jars of spice blends like dukkah, za'atar, etc., to add variety to your vegetable dishes. You can serve raw cauliflower with a yogurt-herb sauce one day, then make roasted cauliflower with Parmesan and dukkah a couple of days later. Varying the flavors in this way will ensure it doesn't feel like you're eating the same thing again.

Enjoy and savor these moments—they're precious and will remain in your heart forever.

SUMMER BITES

Serves 3–4

ACTIVE TIME
15 minutes

COOKING TIME
About 30 minutes

INGREDIENTS
1 zucchini
1 golden zucchini
2 peaches
3 apricots
4 figs
Extra-virgin olive oil
Fleur de sel
Freshly ground pepper
A few fresh rosemary and thyme sprigs
5–7 oz. (150–200 g) feta, cut into cubes
Tiny sprigs assorted fresh herbs (rosemary,
    thyme, lavender, dwarf basil, etc.),
    to garnish

1. Wash the zucchini, golden zucchini, and fruits. Trim the ends off both types
   of zucchini and cut each one lengthwise into thin slices, ideally using a mandoline
   (but watch your fingers!).
2. Heat a little olive oil in a large skillet or grill pan over high heat. Add the
   vegetable slices in a single layer. Season with fleur de sel and pepper and cook
   until the slices are golden and scorched on both sides. Remove from the pan.
3. Cut the peaches and apricots in half and remove the pits. Cut the figs in half.
   Brush the cut sides with a little olive oil.
4. Set the fruits cut side down in a skillet over high heat, with rosemary and thyme
   sprigs scattered around for extra flavor. Cook for about 2 minutes until lightly
   golden.
5. Place a cube of feta on one end of each zucchini slice and roll the slices up
   around the cheese. Secure with toothpicks. Top each fruit half with a feta cube.
6. Warm the summer bites in a skillet over medium heat for 2 minutes. Arrange
   on a serving plate, garnish with tiny sprigs of fresh herbs, season with pepper,
   and serve.

HONEYDEW MELON AND TARRAGON JUICE

Serves 3

ACTIVE TIME
10–15 minutes

INGREDIENTS
1¼ lb. (550 g) honeydew melon,
  rind and seeds removed
½ tsp honey
Juice of 1 lime
4–5 sprigs fresh tarragon, divided
12 large ice cubes, divided
Lime slices, preferably organic, to decorate

1. Cut the melon into pieces. Place in a blender with the honey, lime juice, and leaves of 3 tarragon sprigs.
2. Add half the ice cubes to the blender and blend until smooth.
3. Divide the remaining ice cubes between 3 large glasses. Pour in the juice. Decorate each drink with small tarragon sprigs and lime slices. Serve immediately.

KITCHEN NOTES: This delicious, refreshing juice is perfect for a hot summer's day! You can also experiment with other fruit and herb combinations, such as watermelon and mint, peach and basil, or strawberry and verbena. Or try vegetable juices like cucumber and rosemary.

GRILLED SARDINES WITH LEMON-MINT SAUCE

Serves 3

ACTIVE TIME
8–10 minutes

COOKING TIME
8–10 minutes

INGREDIENTS
For the sauce
1 small preserved lemon
Juice of ½ lemon
Leaves of 6 sprigs fresh mint
1 handful pecan halves
3–4 tbsp extra-virgin olive oil
Fleur de sel and freshly ground pepper

For the sardines
12 sardines
Fleur de sel

To serve
Country bread

1. Place all the sauce ingredients in a food processor and process until smooth. Add more olive oil and a little extra lemon juice if you want a thinner consistency. Season with fleur de sel and pepper to taste.
2. Grill the sardines over a wood fire for 4–5 minutes on each side. Sprinkle them with fleur de sel, and serve with the sauce and country bread.

KITCHEN NOTES: The lemon-mint sauce is also delicious over pasta or served with grilled vegetables.

TOMATO AND SMOKED BACON SALAD

Serves 4, as a starter

ACTIVE TIME
10 minutes

COOKING TIME
12 minutes

INGREDIENTS
3½ oz. (100 g) thinly sliced smoked bacon
2 shallots, finely chopped
1 tbsp Dijon mustard
4 tbsp extra-virgin olive oil
3 tbsp red wine vinegar
3½ oz. (100 g) Roquefort, crumbled
4–5 assorted tomatoes
Fresh chives, snipped

1. Cook the bacon in an ungreased skillet over medium heat, until browned and crisp. Remove using a slotted spoon and drain on paper towels. Set aside.
2. Add the shallots to the same skillet and sauté until softened and browned. Stir in the mustard, olive oil, and vinegar. Remove from the heat and add the Roquefort.
3. Wash and core the tomatoes. Cut them into wedges and place in a salad bowl. Add the shallot-Roquefort mixture and toss lightly together.
4. Sprinkle over the chives. Break the bacon into pieces and scatter over the top.

KITCHEN NOTES: For a note of freshness, you can add some diced cucumber and/or a little lemon.

PEACH, ZUCCHINI, AND BURRATA PIZZA

Makes 2 pizzas, to serve 4

ACTIVE TIME
20 minutes, plus making
  the pizza dough

COOKING TIME
25 minutes per pizza

INGREDIENTS
For the arugula pesto
5¼ oz. (150 g) arugula
Scant ½ cup (2¾ oz./80 g)
  grated Parmesan
1 clove garlic
½ cup (2½ oz./70 g) toasted
  blanched hazelnuts
  or almonds
¾ cup (200 ml) extra-virgin
  olive oil
Fleur de sel and freshly
  ground pepper

For the pizzas
1 quantity pizza dough
  (see pp. 38–39)
6 tbsp arugula pesto
  (see left)
1–2 zucchini
2 peaches
Generous ½ cup (2 oz./60 g)
  freshly grated Parmesan
8 oz. (250 g) burrata
Arugula
Five-peppercorn mix,
  crushed

1. Preheat the oven to 375°F (190°C/Gas Mark 5).
2. To prepare the arugula pesto, place all the ingredients except the olive oil in a food processor and process until finely chopped. With the processor running, gradually add the oil until well combined and smooth. Season with fleur de sel and pepper to taste.
3. To assemble the pizza, cut the pizza dough in half and stretch or roll each piece into a disk.
4. Spread a thin layer of pesto over the dough, leaving a narrow border all the way around.
5. Wash the zucchini and slice it thinly crosswise. Arrange the slices over the pesto, overlapping them slightly.
6. Wash the peaches, then halve, pit, and cut them into ½-in. (1-cm) slices. Arrange them over the zucchini. Sprinkle over the Parmesan.
7. Bake one pizza at a time for 15–20 minutes. If the crust is browning too slowly, switch to the broiler setting for the final 3 minutes.
8. Scatter over pieces of burrata, arugula, and crushed peppercorns. Serve immediately.

GRILLED PEACH AND AVOCADO SALAD WITH GOAT CHEESE

Serves 6

ACTIVE TIME
20 minutes

COOKING TIME
15 minutes

INGREDIENTS
4 yellow peaches
Extra-virgin olive oil for
    drizzling, plus 3 tbsp for
    the dressing
4 ripe but firm avocados
2 figs, quartered
Finely grated zest and juice
    of 1 lemon, preferably
    organic
7 oz. (200 g) fresh goat
    cheese
1–2 shallots, finely chopped
2 tbsp apple balsamic
    vinegar (see Kitchen Note)
    or regular balsamic
    vinegar
1 handful toasted almonds,
    roughly chopped
Assorted fresh herb leaves
    (arugula, basil, oregano,
    etc.)
1 pinch piment d'Espelette
Salt and freshly ground
    pepper

1. Heat a grill to medium (if you don't have a lower-heat grill, use a grill pan or skillet).
2. Wash the peaches, remove the pits, and cut them, unpeeled, into ¾–1¼-in. (2–3-cm) slices. Place in a large bowl, drizzle with olive oil, and gently stir until the slices are coated.
3. Cut the avocados in half, remove the pits and skin, and cut each half lengthwise into three slices. Drizzle with olive oil and gently turn to coat evenly.
4. Grill the peach and avocado slices for 3–4 minutes on each side, until charred in places. Check them regularly to ensure they do not burn.
5. Arrange the peach and avocado slices with the fig quarters on a serving dish. Sprinkle with the lemon zest. Crumble the goat cheese over the top.
6. To make the dressing, whisk the shallots, 3 tbsp olive oil, vinegar, and lemon juice together in a bowl. Season with salt and pepper. Drizzle over the salad.
7. Scatter over the almonds and herbs, sprinkle with the piment d'Espelette, and serve.

KITCHEN NOTES: I use La Pommée, an artisanal apple balsamic vinegar made by Maison Le Paulmier in Normandy.

CARROT, CILANTRO, AND COCONUT CREAM FLAN

Serves 8, as a side dish

ACTIVE TIME
25–30 minutes

COOKING TIME
1 hour 40 minutes

INGREDIENTS
3⅓ lb. (1.5 kg) carrots
1 tbsp butter
2 yellow onions, finely chopped
8 eggs
1 bunch fresh cilantro,
    finely chopped and divided
1 tsp ground coriander
2 pinches grated or ground nutmeg
1⅓ cups (330 ml) coconut cream
1 handful toasted hazelnuts, roughly
    chopped
Edible flowers (optional)
Salt and freshly ground pepper

1. Peel the carrots and slice them crosswise into ¾–1¼-in. (2–3-cm) rounds. Steam for 30 minutes until tender.
2. Meanwhile, melt the butter in a skillet over low heat, add the onions and a pinch of salt, and cook until softened and lightly browned.
3. Transfer the carrots and onions to a food processor and pulse to a puree.
4. Whisk the eggs together in a large bowl, then add half the chopped cilantro and the ground coriander and nutmeg. Whisk to blend, then whisk in the coconut cream, followed by the carrot-onion puree. Season with salt and pepper.
5. Preheat the oven to 300°F (150°C/Gas Mark 2).
6. Place a baking dish in a hot-water bath and pour the mixture into the dish. Bake for 45 minutes, then increase the oven temperature to 340°F (170°C/Gas Mark 3) and bake for an additional 10–15 minutes. The consistency should be set but not too firm, and the tip of a knife inserted into the center should come out clean.
7. Just before serving, sprinkle over the hazelnuts, remaining cilantro, and edible flowers, if using. Serve warm or cold.

COCONUT CHICKEN

Serves 4

ACTIVE TIME
15 minutes

MARINATING TIME
20 minutes

COOKING TIME
35–40 minutes

INGREDIENTS
5 limes, preferably organic, divided
1 heaping tsp massalé spice blend
   (see Kitchen Notes)
2 tbsp extra-virgin olive oil
1 clove garlic, finely chopped
4 chicken legs, preferably free-range
Scant 1 cup (2¾ oz./80 g) unsweetened
   shredded coconut
A few sprigs cilantro, roughly chopped
Salt and freshly ground pepper

1. Finely grate the zest of 3 limes, then juice them.
2. In a large bowl, combine the lime zest and juice with the massalé spice blend, olive oil, and garlic. Season with salt and pepper, add the chicken legs, and turn the legs over until they are coated on all sides. Let marinate for at least 20 minutes.
3. Preheat the oven to 400°F (200°C/Gas Mark 6).
4. Add the coconut to the chicken and turn the legs over until they are well coated.
5. In an oven-safe skillet, brown the chicken legs for 3–4 minutes on each side over medium heat. Place in the oven and bake for 25 minutes, turning the legs halfway through the cooking time. Check the meat for doneness and bake for an additional 5–10 minutes, if necessary.
6. Quarter the remaining limes and tuck them around the chicken, sprinkle with the cilantro, and serve.

KITCHEN NOTES: Massalé is a spice mix from the island of Réunion that is a blend of coriander, fenugreek, turmeric, oregano, cumin, ginger, chili pepper, nutmeg, cardamom, and cloves. It is available from specialty food stores but if you cannot find it, use curry powder instead.
This chicken is excellent with ginger-scented boiled rice and mango or apricot chutney.

SPINACH PIE

Serves 6–8

ACTIVE TIME
20 minutes

COOLING TIME
30 minutes

COOKING TIME
40–45 minutes

INGREDIENTS
3 tbsp (1¾ oz./50 g) unsalted butter
2 shallots, finely chopped
2 cloves garlic, finely chopped
3 tbsp (1 oz./30 g) all-purpose flour
1⅓ cups (320 ml) whole milk
1½ cups (5 oz./150 g) grated Parmesan
1¼ lb. (550 g) frozen spinach, thawed and
    squeezed dry
2 round sheets puff pastry (about 12½ in./
    32 cm in diameter), preferably all-butter
1 egg, beaten
Salt and freshly ground pepper

1. Melt the butter in a saucepan over low heat. Add the shallots, garlic, and a pinch of salt, and cook for 2 minutes. Stirring continuously, add the flour and cook for about 30 seconds. Gradually whisk in the milk and cook for 2–3 minutes, until the mixture thickens and becomes smooth.
2. Remove from the heat, stir in the Parmesan and spinach, and season to taste with salt and pepper. Transfer to a bowl and let cool completely.
3. Preheat the oven to 400°F (200°C/Gas Mark 6).
4. Line a 9-10-in. (23-25-cm) tart pan with one of the pastry sheets. Spread the spinach mixture over the pastry and cover with the second sheet. Press the pastry edges together and seal them using the tines of a fork.
   Make several small holes in the top to let steam escape. Brush the pastry with the beaten egg to glaze, sprinkle with pepper, and bake for 35–40 minutes, until golden brown.

KITCHEN NOTES: This pie is delicious served hot or at room temperature, with a fresh green salad on the side.

FETA AND ZUCCHINI PASTA

You'll have undoubtedly seen the viral baked feta and cherry tomato pasta recipe posted by a Finnish food blogger. I was curious to try it with zucchini—and it was a huge hit!

Serves 4

ACTIVE TIME
15 minutes

COOKING TIME
30– 35 minutes

INGREDIENTS
2–3 zucchini
About 20 cherry tomatoes
2 shallots, finely chopped
2 cloves garlic, finely chopped
3–4 sprigs fresh thyme, divided
Extra-virgin olive oil
7 oz. (200 g) feta
1 lb. (500 g) dried pasta of your choice
Fleur de sel
Grated Parmesan (optional)
Salt and freshly ground pepper

1. Preheat the oven to 400°F (200°C/Gas Mark 6).
2. Wash the zucchini and cherry tomatoes. Trim and cut the zucchini into ½-in. (12-mm) cubes and place them in a baking dish large enough to hold the pasta once cooked. Add the cherry tomatoes, shallots, garlic, and the leaves of 2 thyme sprigs. Drizzle with olive oil, and stir until everything is well coated with oil.
3. Place the feta in one whole piece in the center of the vegetables, drizzle olive oil over the top of it, and bake for 30–35 minutes, until the vegetables are tender and the feta is pale golden.
4. Meanwhile, cook the pasta in a large pan of boiling salted water for 1 minute less than the time indicated on the package. Drain.
5. Remove the dish from the oven. Break up the feta into small pieces, or mash it with a fork, and toss with the vegetables. Stir in the hot pasta, season with fleur de sel and pepper to taste, and stir in the leaves from the remaining thyme sprigs. Finally, add the Parmesan, if you wish.

MINT SORBET

Makes 1 qt. (1 liter)

ACTIVE TIME
30 minutes

COOKING TIME
10 minutes

CHILLING TIME
12 hours

INGREDIENTS
1¼ cups (300 ml) boiling water
1½ cups (10½ oz./300 g) superfine sugar
Leaves of 5–6 fresh mint sprigs
2 cups (500 ml) cold water
Juice of ½ lemon
Limoncello or chocolate chips (optional)

1. One day ahead, combine the boiling water and sugar in a large bowl, stirring until the sugar dissolves.
2. Add the mint leaves and crush them with a fork to release their flavor.
3. Let cool for 10 minutes, then stir in the cold water. Cover and refrigerate overnight.
4. The following day, remove the mint leaves and add the lemon juice.
5. Churn in an ice cream or sorbet maker for 25 minutes, or according to the manufacturer's instructions. Store in the freezer.
6. Serve each guest with a generous scoop of sorbet. If you wish, pour a little Limoncello into each serving dish (very refreshing after dinner), or sprinkle chocolate chips over and around each scoop (for a flavor reminiscent of After Eights).

KITCHEN NOTES: This sorbet will keep for up to two weeks in the freezer in an airtight container. It is also delicious served with fresh blackberries and blueberries.

FROSTED PISTACHIO CAKE

Serves 10

ACTIVE TIME
25–30 minutes

COOKING TIME
40–45 minutes

COOLING TIME
25–30 minutes

CHILLING TIME
15 minutes

INGREDIENTS
For the cake
Butter and flour, for greasing

2 cups (9 oz./250 g) shelled pistachios
2¼ cups (10 oz./280 g) all-purpose flour
1 scant tbsp (11 g) baking powder
2 pinches baking soda
1 generous pinch fleur de sel
1½ sticks (6 oz./180 g) unsalted butter, diced, at room temperature
¾ cup (5 oz./150 g) superfine sugar
⅔ cup (5¼ oz./150 g) brown sugar
4 egg whites
½ cup (4¼ oz./120 g) crème fraîche

1 tsp bitter almond extract
Scant 1 cup (240 ml) low-fat milk

For the frosting and decoration
1 cup (9 oz./250 g) cream cheese, at room temperature
7 tbsp (4 oz./110 g) unsalted butter, diced, at room temperature
3 cups (14 oz./400 g) confectioners' sugar
Shelled pistachios, roughly chopped
Assorted berries and fresh herbs

1. Preheat the oven to 350°F (180°C/Gas Mark 4). Grease a 9½-in. (24-cm) springform pan with butter and dust with flour.
2. Pulse the pistachios into fine crumbs using a food processor. Place in a mixing bowl and stir in the flour, baking powder, baking soda, and fleur de sel until combined.
3. In a separate large bowl, beat together the butter, superfine sugar, and brown sugar. Using an electric beater, whisk in the egg whites one at a time, then whisk at high speed for 2–3 minutes until light and creamy. Stir in the crème fraîche and almond extract. Gradually fold in the dry ingredients. Stir in the milk.
4. Transfer the batter to the pan. Bake for 40–45 minutes, or until the tip of a knife inserted into the center comes out clean. Let cool for about 10 minutes before removing from the pan. Transfer to a serving plate and let cool for 15–20 minutes.
5. Meanwhile, prepare the frosting. Stir together the cream cheese and butter until smooth, then gradually stir in the confectioners' sugar. Chill for about 15 minutes.
6. Spread a thick layer of frosting over the top of the cake and decorate as you wish with pistachios, berries, and herbs.

KITCHEN NOTES: The undecorated frosted cake can be stored for 2–3 days in the refrigerator; take it out about 30 minutes before serving and decorate.

FALL

WARM AUTUMNAL COLORS AND COZY GATHERINGS

After the long, lazy days of summer, fall sneaks up on us. The leaves on the trees turn yellow, ocher, and red. We pull out our blankets and sweaters, and can't wait to light the first log fire of the season. Our homes are decorated with all sorts of squash, and comforting dishes make a comeback. Everything seems to slow down and become cozy.

FLOWERS
Dahlias, Japanese anemones, fall-blooming camellias and hydrangeas, proteas.

TABLE DECOR
Apples; dried flowers and leaves; vintage quilts; thicker, heavier materials such as glass, ceramics, and metals; dried corncobs; squash-shaped bread rolls; assorted squash. Fall brings with it the last harvests before the winter vegetables appear. Use warm colors, or else soft, neutral tones. At farmers' markets, you will find stunning squash varieties in soft tones to decorate your table, such as Baby Boo, Hungarian Blue, and white pattypan.

PLACE CARD AND GIFT IDEAS
A dried apple slice, cinnamon stick, and small crystal attached to each drinking glass using a ribbon; bandanas that you've hand-embroidered; toffee apples; bottles of farmhouse cider.

PARTY IDEAS
Make a large pot of hot mulled apple cider or a signature cocktail using cinnamon and figs. Prepare a big cheese board along with other little culinary treats—perfect for an *apéritif dinatoire* (an informal cocktail dinner). Remember to have plenty of blankets on hand.

Pumpkins, apples, and leaves are typically used for autumnal decor, but you can arrange them any number of ways. For instance, you can turn apples into candle holders (see the DIY version in my first book, *Miss Maggie's Kitchen: Relaxed French Entertaining*), or write guests' names on leaves and use them as place cards.

AUTUMN UNDER THE APPLE TREES

· Use apples as candle holders, empty glass bottles (beer, wine) as vases or candlesticks, baby pumpkins in lieu of place cards, and wooden crates as coffee tables. Let your creativity guide you.
· Fall is the perfect season for bringing branches of colorful leaves into your home. I'm a fan of floral arrangements that don't look too fussy or labored. I have a few vases, but I especially like repurposing other containers, such as old earthenware jars, jugs, antique silver champagne buckets, and so on, as I find them more original. You can also experiment with hanging a maple branch over your table, with or without string lights.

A WESTERN AUTUMN

· Combine autumnal colors such as brown and ocher with blue, pink, and yellow, to recall the golden light at the end of summer. Use tablecloths made of heavy fabrics, bandanas as napkins, and dried flowers. Imagine a meal with family and friends after a long day of horseback riding in the great outdoors.

A NORDIC AUTUMN

· Use ceramics, an abundance of one particular seasonal product (pears, for instance), metal, and linen or thick cotton—all in neutral colors. Opt for various shades of white and gray, and a return to essential, bold pieces.

A FEW TIPS IF YOU CELEBRATE THANKSGIVING:

· Accept help, whether it be with the shopping or the preparation of certain dishes.
· Plan your menu in advance, so you can decide what to prepare ahead of time and determine what needs to be made on the day.
· Get started on the table setting one or two days ahead. This will give you time to make adjustments or any final purchases. For the tablecloth, consider repurposing a vintage quilt or plaid blanket.
· Serve the meal buffet-style—it's much simpler than table service, and guests can help themselves according to their personal tastes.
· Offer each guest a little gift, a note to express your gratitude for their friendship, a souvenir photo, etc.

GREENGAGE PLUM, BACON, AND BURRATA CROSTINI

Makes 8 medium-sized crostini

ACTIVE TIME
15 minutes

COOKING TIME
15 minutes

INGREDIENTS
8 slices country bread
12 greengage (Reine-Claude) plums, or
   another sweet plum of your choice
Extra-virgin olive oil
Apple balsamic vinegar (see Kitchen Notes)
   or regular balsamic vinegar
Fleur de sel
5 oz. (150 g) smoked bacon
8 oz. (250 g) burrata
Leaves of a few sprigs fresh mint, chopped
Freshly ground pepper

1. Toast the bread slices on both sides and set aside.
2. Wash the plums, cut them in half, and remove the pits. Brush the cut sides with olive oil, drizzle with balsamic vinegar, and sear the cut sides in a grill pan or over a barbecue grill until browned. Sprinkle with fleur de sel, remove from the pan or grill, and set aside.
3. Cook the bacon in an ungreased skillet over medium heat until golden brown and crisp. Remove, drain on paper towels, and let cool.
4. Break the bacon into small pieces. Place 3 plum halves on each slice of toast and top with a little burrata. Sprinkle over the bacon bits and mint, season with fleur de sel and pepper, and serve.

KITCHEN NOTES: I use La Pommée, an artisanal apple balsamic vinegar made by Maison Le Paulmier in Normandy.

CORN GAZPACHO

Serves 4

ACTIVE TIME
20 minutes

COOKING TIME
10 minutes

CHILLING TIME
30 minutes

INGREDIENTS
3 ears of corn, husks removed
Extra-virgin olive oil
3 yellow tomatoes
1 yellow bell pepper, deseeded
½ cucumber
1 yellow onion, finely chopped
2 tbsp white wine vinegar or cider vinegar
½ red onion
Small bunch fresh basil leaves, shredded
Fleur de sel
Salt and freshly ground pepper

1. Cut the kernels off the corncobs. Heat a little olive oil and salt in a skillet and gently sauté the kernels over low heat, until golden brown and caramelized. Remove from the skillet and let cool.
2. Wash the tomatoes and bell pepper, and cut them into pieces. Cut the ½ cucumber in half widthwise, then peel one half and cut it into pieces; set aside the other half.
3. Place the tomatoes, bell pepper, cucumber, and yellow onion in a blender with three-quarters of the corn kernels. Add 4–5 tablespoons of olive oil and the vinegar. Season with salt and pepper.
4. Process to a puree. Taste and adjust the seasoning and consistency, by diluting with a little water, as needed. Chill for 30 minutes.
5. Chop the remaining, unpeeled cucumber into small dice. Do the same with the red onion. Place in a bowl with the basil and remaining corn kernels. Drizzle with olive oil and season with a little fleur de sel and pepper.
6. Just before serving, spoon the gazpacho into four soup plates and garnish with the diced vegetable mixture.

KITCHEN NOTES: You can also serve this gazpacho with garlic-rubbed crostini sprinkled with lemon zest.

ARTICHOKES WITH OLIVES AND FETA

Serves 4–6, as a starter or side dish

ACTIVE TIME
10 minutes

COOKING TIME
30–35 minutes

INGREDIENTS
Extra-virgin olive oil
1 shallot, finely chopped
12 oz. (350 g) artichoke hearts canned
    in water (drained weight)
1–2 cloves garlic, finely chopped
Juice and finely grated zest of 1 lemon,
    preferably organic
1 tbsp fennel seeds
3–4 fresh thyme sprigs, divided
10½ oz. (300 g) assorted olives
2 tbsp capers
5 oz. (150 g) feta, crumbled
Fleur de sel
Salt and freshly ground pepper

1. Heat a little olive oil in a skillet. Add the shallot, season with a little salt, and fry over medium heat for 2 minutes, until softened.
2. Quarter the well-drained artichoke hearts, add to the skillet, and sauté for about 7–8 minutes, until golden.
3. Add the garlic, lemon juice, fennel seeds, and the leaves of 2–3 thyme sprigs. Stir to combine and cook for 2–3 minutes.
4. Stir in the olives and capers. Reduce the heat to low and cook gently for about 20 minutes.
5. Toss in the lemon zest and feta, and season with fleur de sel and pepper. Break the remaining thyme sprig into pieces, scatter them over the dish to garnish, and serve.

KITCHEN NOTES: These artichokes make a delicious starter or side dish, or can be served on slices of toasted country bread at cocktail hour.

GRAPE AND FIG PIZZA

Makes 2 pizzas, to serve 4

ACTIVE TIME
15 minutes, plus making the pizza dough

COOKING TIME
20 minutes

INGREDIENTS
1 quantity pizza dough (see recipe pp. 38–39)
6 tbsp basil pesto (store-bought
   or homemade)
2 oz. (60 g) Parmesan, grated
6–7 fresh figs, halved or quartered
2–3 bunches grapes
5 oz. (150 g) thinly sliced speck
9 oz. (250 g) burrata, cut into pieces
Arugula
Truffle oil
Five-peppercorn blend, crushed

1. Preheat the oven to 375°F (190°C/Gas Mark 5).
2. Divide the pizza dough in half. Roll or stretch each half across a sheet of parchment paper to make two disks with a thickness of about ¼ in. (5 mm). Slide onto baking sheets.
3. Spread each base thinly with 3 tbsp pesto, leaving a slight border all the way around. Sprinkle over the Parmesan and bake for 10 minutes.
4. Remove the pizzas from the oven and top with the figs and grapes. Bake for an additional 5–7 minutes, then switch the oven to broiler setting and broil for 3–4 minutes.
5. Remove from the oven and scatter over the speck and burrata. Top with arugula, drizzle with truffle oil, and sprinkle with the crushed peppercorns.

ROAST CHICKEN LEGS WITH GRAPES

Serves 4

ACTIVE TIME
10 minutes

COOKING TIME
40 minutes

INGREDIENTS
3 tbsp (1¾ oz./50 g) unsalted butter
4 chicken legs, preferably free-range
3 tbsp apple balsamic vinegar (see Kitchen
    Notes) or regular balsamic vinegar
Extra-virgin olive oil
2 yellow onions, chopped
4–5 small bunches assorted grapes
4–5 sprigs fresh rosemary, to garnish
Salt and freshly ground pepper

1. Preheat the oven to 375°F (190°C/Gas Mark 5).
2. Melt the butter in an oven-safe skillet over medium-high heat.
3. Season the chicken legs with salt, place them in the skillet, and pour the vinegar over them. Cook for about 4–5 minutes on each side, until the legs are browned. Remove them from the skillet and transfer to a plate.
4. Add a little olive oil to the skillet and fry the onions with a pinch of salt over medium heat, until softened. Place the grapes over the onions.
5. Arrange the chicken legs over the grapes and place the skillet in the oven for 20–25 minutes. Check the chicken for doneness and place back in the oven for a few more minutes, if needed (the cooking time will depend on the thickness of the legs).
6. Serve garnished with rosemary sprigs.

KITCHEN NOTES: I use La Pommée, an artisanal apple balsamic vinegar made by Maison Le Paulmier in Normandy.
A side of mashed potatoes or zucchini makes a great accompaniment to this chicken dish.

VEGGIE TAGINE

Serves 5–6

ACTIVE TIME
25 minutes

COOKING TIME
1¼–1½ hours

INGREDIENTS
For the tagine
½ butternut squash, peeled
  and seeded
2 carrots, peeled
2 zucchini, washed
1 eggplant, washed
Extra-virgin olive oil
1 red onion, chopped

1 shallot, chopped
3 cloves garlic, finely
  chopped
2 tsp tomato paste
1 tbsp ground cinnamon
1½ tsp ground cumin
1½ tsp ground coriander
1 tbsp coriander seeds
2 tbsp honey
Scant 2 cups (480 ml)
  vegetable broth
About 20 green olives
Salt and freshly ground
  pepper

For the couscous
1⅔ cups (10½ oz./300 g)
  couscous
3 tbsp (1¾ oz./50 g) lightly
  salted butter, diced
1–2 tsp ground cinnamon
About 1 cup (2¾–3½ oz./
  80–100 g) toasted almond
  slices
⅓ cup (2 oz./60 g) golden
  raisins (sultanas)

To serve
½ bunch fresh cilantro,
  chopped
½ bunch fresh mint,
  chopped

1. To prepare the tagine, trim and cut the squash, carrots, zucchini, and eggplant into bite-size pieces.
2. Heat a little olive oil in a large sauté pan and cook the squash, carrots, zucchini, eggplant, red onion, and shallot with a pinch of salt over medium heat for about 10 minutes, stirring occasionally, until the vegetables are just beginning to soften and brown on the edges.
3. Add the garlic, tomato paste, cinnamon, cumin, ground coriander, and coriander seeds. Stir and let cook for 3 minutes, then stir in the honey and broth. Add the olives. Cover the pan, reduce the heat to low, and let simmer for 40–45 minutes, until the vegetables are tender. Taste and season with salt and pepper.
4. Meanwhile, prepare the couscous according to the package instructions. Stir in the butter until it melts, then stir in the cinnamon, almonds, and golden raisins. Season with salt and pepper to taste.
5. Spoon the couscous and tagine into serving dishes. Just before serving, sprinkle the chopped cilantro and mint over the tagine.

KITCHEN NOTES: This recipe can be made all year long, using whatever vegetables are in season or take your fancy.

JACQUES'S BEEF BOURGUIGNON

Serves 6–8

ACTIVE TIME
25 minutes

COOKING TIME
About 3½ hours

INGREDIENTS
4–5 tbsp canola oil
3 lb. (1.5 kg) stewing beef, cut into 2-in. (5-cm) cubes

10½ oz. (300 g) smoked bacon, cut into lardons
1 large yellow onion, finely chopped
3 cloves garlic, finely chopped
1 bottle red wine (Chianti or Bordeaux)
3 tbsp tomato paste
2 cups (500 ml) beef stock
2 bay leaves
4 sprigs fresh thyme

1½ tbsp unsalted butter, divided
14 oz. (400 g) pearl onions, peeled (and halved, if large)
14 oz. (400 g) assorted mushrooms (button, girolle, chanterelle, etc.)
3 carrots, peeled and sliced thinly crosswise
2 tbsp all-purpose flour (optional)
Salt and freshly ground pepper

1. Heat half the oil in a large Dutch oven and sear the beef cubes in batches over high heat, removing them as they brown and adding more oil as necessary. When all the meat has browned, place it all back in the pot. Add the bacon and onion, and cook for 3–4 minutes over medium heat. Stir in the garlic, wine, tomato paste, beef stock, bay leaves, and thyme and bring to a simmer, scraping the bottom of the pot to incorporate any meat juices sticking to it. Cover and let simmer for 15 minutes.

2. Preheat the oven to 300°F (150°C/Gas Mark 2). Place the covered pot in the oven and cook for 2½ hours.

3. Meanwhile, melt 1 tablespoon butter in a large skillet, add the pearl onions, and sauté over medium heat until browned. In a separate skillet, melt the remaining butter, add the mushrooms, and sauté over medium heat until browned. Set aside.

4. Remove the pot from the oven and add the sliced carrots, pearl onions, and mushrooms. Let simmer, partially covered, for 30 minutes, until the beef and vegetables are tender. Taste and adjust the seasoning, if necessary.

5. If you wish to thicken the sauce, place the flour in a bowl and whisk in about 1 tablespoon cold water using a fork until smooth. Gradually whisk in 3 tablespoons of the sauce from the pot, then pour this mixture into the pot and stir until the sauce slowly thickens.

KITCHEN NOTES: I like to serve this beef Bourgignon with boiled potatoes.

MAC & CHEESE

Serves 3–4

ACTIVE TIME
10 minutes

COOKING TIME
10–15 minutes

INGREDIENTS
8 oz. (240 g) macaroni (straight or elbow)
4 tbsp (2 oz./60 g) unsalted butter
½ cup (2 oz./60 g) all-purpose flour
Scant 2 cups (480 ml) whole milk
7 oz. (200 g) good-quality sharp
    or extra-sharp Cheddar, grated
2 sprigs fresh thyme
Salt and freshly ground pepper

1. Cook the macaroni in a large pan of boiling salted water for 7–8 minutes, or until al dente.
2. Meanwhile, melt the butter in a saucepan over medium heat. Stir in the flour until smooth and cook for 1 minute. Gradually stir in the milk and bring to a boil, stirring continuously, until the mixture thickens and becomes smooth. Remove the pan from the heat and stir in the Cheddar until melted. Season to taste with salt and pepper.
3. When the macaroni is cooked, drain and place it in a large bowl. Pour over the sauce and stir with a wooden spoon until the macaroni is well coated with the sauce. Garnish with the thyme sprigs and serve.

KITCHEN NOTES: This recipe is infinitely adaptable, so go ahead and mix it up! You can combine two cheeses (Cheddar and Parmesan, for instance), or toss the macaroni with add-ins like crisp bacon bits, roast chicken breast, ham, cooked vegetables such as mushrooms, or even a few drops of white truffle oil.

COCONUT CAKE

Serves 8–10

ACTIVE TIME
20 minutes

COOKING TIME
45 minutes–1 hour

COOLING TIME
20 minutes

INGREDIENTS
Butter and flour for the pan
1 stick plus 2 tsp (4½ oz./125 g) unsalted
   butter
½ cup (3½ oz./100 g) brown sugar
3 eggs
1⅔ cups (7 oz./200 g) all-purpose flour
1 scant tbsp (11 g) baking powder
1 pinch baking soda
1 pinch fleur de sel
Scant ½ cup (100 ml) whole milk
1¾ cups (5 oz./140 g) unsweetened
   shredded coconut, divided
Generous ½ cup (6½ oz./185 g) blueberry
   jam (or another jam of your choice)

1. Preheat the oven to 375°F (190°C/Gas Mark 5). Grease a standard loaf pan with butter and dust it with flour.
2. Gently melt the butter and pour it into a mixing bowl. Stir in the brown sugar. Whisk in the eggs one at a time.
3. In a separate bowl, mix together the flour, baking powder, baking soda, and fleur de sel.
4. Using a spatula, mix the dry ingredients into the egg mixture. Gradually add the milk to make a smooth batter. Fold in 1 generous cup (3½ oz./100 g) of the shredded coconut.
5. Pour the batter into the prepared loaf pan. Bake for 45–50 minutes, or until the tip of a knife inserted into the center of the cake comes out clean. Bake for an additional 10 minutes, if needed.
6. Turn the cake out of the pan onto a wire rack and let cool for about 20 minutes. Spread the jam over the top of the cake and sprinkle over the remaining coconut. Serve warm or at room temperature.

PEARS IN PUFF PASTRY

Serves 4

ACTIVE TIME
20–25 minutes

COOKING TIME
25 minutes

INGREDIENTS
2 ripe but firm pears
1 tsp lemon juice
2 tsp brown sugar
Ground cinnamon (optional)
3 tbsp jam, such as apricot, fig, or mirabelle plum
1 sheet puff pastry, preferably all-butter
Granulated sugar (optional)

1. Preheat the oven to 375°F (190°C/Gas Mark 5).
2. Wash the pears and cut them in half lengthwise. Brush the cut sides with a little lemon juice, then sprinkle with the brown sugar and a little ground cinnamon, if you wish.
3. Line a baking sheet with parchment paper and place the pears, cut side down, on it. Spoon a little jam onto the rounded side of each pear.
4. Roll out the puff pastry to a thickness of about ¼ in. (5 mm) and lay it over the pear halves. Using a sharp knife, cut the pastry around each half, so it is completely covered with a pastry shell. You can use the dough trimmings to cut out fun shapes, such as small branches and leaves, to decorate the shells. Brush the shapes with a little water and press them gently onto the pastry shells to attach them.
5. Cut 2 small slits in each pastry shell to let steam escape. Sprinkle them with cinnamon and granulated sugar, if you wish. Bake for 20–25 minutes, until the pastry is golden brown.
6. Let cool for 1–2 minutes, then carefully turn each pear half over. Serve warm or at room temperature.

KITCHEN NOTES: The pears can be served with a scoop of ice cream, granola, or chocolate chips.
You can also make this recipe using other fruits, such as apples, peaches, or apricots—the choice is yours.

WINTER

HAPPY HOLIDAYS WITHOUT THE STRESS

Every year, the frenzy of the holiday season can leave us feeling
a little frazzled. Here are a few reminders and planning tips
to help you enjoy this festive time of year as serenely as possible.
This timeline was made with Christmas in mind, but it can easily
be adapted to suit any holiday.

FLOWERS
Beautyberry, Christmas roses, mimosa
flowers, buttercups, anemones, amaryllis,
hyacinths, poinsettias in assorted colors
(red, white, pink, peach), mistletoe,
eucalyptus branches.

TABLE DECOR
A centerpiece in shades of green and white
to evoke the forest; warm, joyful colors;
a chic British look; a pale color palette
for a New Year filled with lightness.

PLACE CARD AND GIFT IDEAS
A homemade wreath;
Christmas cookies or fortune cookies;
a sachet of potpourri; a homemade
tin of tea; dried citrus slices.

PARTY IDEAS
A disco ball; a large pitcher of eggnog;
a great festive playlist.

END OF OCTOBER
· Start thinking about your holiday cards:
  make a list of recipients, choose a
  design (photo, illustration, something
  homemade with recycled book pages,
  etc.).

SIX WEEKS AHEAD
· Make your wish-list for Santa.

FIRST WEEK OF DECEMBER
· Purchase gifts, wrapping paper, and gift
  tags, and send any long-distance gifts.
· Make an inventory of your decorations:
  what do you have already? What do
  you want to make yourself? Do the
  string lights still work?
· Start thinking about the table setting:
  do you need to order a centerpiece

from your favorite florist? Or will you make one yourself? Can your children help? Is the tablecloth clean and ironed? Do you need to polish any silverware?

· Take your time writing your holiday cards.
· Buy a Christmas tree to fill your home with its wonderful scent.
· Finish concocting your Christmas Eve and Christmas Day menus, and make your shopping lists (see p. 18 for my personal method). It isn't always easy to meet the special dietary requirements of all your guests, so just do your best!
· Order your turkey (for my cooking tips, see the facing page).
· Decorate your home. Hang a beautiful wreath on your door (see p. 134 for my homemade version).
· Start putting together your New Year's Eve party playlist.
· Light pine- and spiced orange-scented candles and make your own potpourri (see p. 134) to fill your home with holiday aromas.

TWO WEEKS AHEAD

· Make sure you have all your gifts and party favors, and finalize your seating plan.
· Clean out your refrigerator—you'll need lots of space!
· Shop for all unperishable items, such as wines, oils, and spices.

· Think about what you'll wear. It can also be fun to ask all your guests to dress according to a certain theme or to wear a certain color.
· Ask your children to sort through their toys and give away any that are in good shape but they're too old for.
· Watch a Christmas movie with your family.

ONE WEEK AHEAD

· Give your house a deep clean, make guest beds, etc.
· Buy batteries for children's toys that will need them.
· Go and see the department store window displays, or take a tour around your neighborhood to look at the Christmas lights. Enjoy a mulled wine at the Christmas market with friends.
· Make Christmas cookies (see recipes pp. 170–71) to give as gifts to your mail carrier, neighbors, friends, children's teachers, etc. Wrap the cookies up in a box with a pretty ribbon.

THREE DAYS AHEAD

· Shop for perishable items.
· Pick up your turkey.
· Start preparing the table setting—not only to get ahead, but also to give yourself plenty of time to make adjustments or buy additional supplies, such as ribbon, without last-minute stress.

TWO DAYS AHEAD

· Prepare any foods you can in advance, such as making pastry for pies or preparing vegetables.
· Pick up flowers or plants from your florist or garden center, or gather branches in the woods.
· Set up a bar area for adults and for children, so your guests can serve themselves. Make sure you have sufficient ice for buckets to chill champagne, white wine, juice, etc., as space is often at a premium in the fridge.
· Donate food and gifts to those in need.

ONE DAY AHEAD

· Finish setting the table and wrapping gifts.
· Determine what time you'll need to put the turkey in the oven and set an alarm on your phone to remind you.
· Prepare treats for breakfast and teatime, such as pecan scones or clementine and pistachio cake (a favorite recipe from my first book).
· Keep (at least) 1 hour free for yourself: have a home "spa" session (put on a facial mask or do your nails), read a book, watch an episode of your favorite series, do a yoga session, take a walk—anything that makes you feel good.

· Relax and sip a cocktail while singing Christmas carols.
· Leave out a glass of milk, cookies, and carrots for Santa and his reindeer.

My turkey roasting tips

· Like chicken, turkey must be at room temperature before it goes into the oven.
· Preheat the oven to 400°F (200°C/Gas Mark 6). Place the turkey in a roasting pan and place in the oven for 20 minutes, then remove, turn the turkey over, and return to the oven for an additional 20 minutes.
· Ensure the turkey is breast-side up, lower the oven temperature to 340°F (170°C/Gas Mark 3), and roast slowly until it is done, basting regularly.
· The chart below gives approximate cooking times, which may vary depending on your oven. If the skin browns too quickly, loosely cover the turkey with aluminum foil.

TURKEY WEIGHT	COOKING TIME
10–12 lb. (4.5–5.5 kg)	2½–3 hours
12–14 lb. (5.5–6.35 kg)	2¾–3½ hours
14–16 lb. (6.35–7.25 kg)	3–3¾ hours
16–19 lb. (7.25–8.6 kg)	3½–4½ hours
20+ lb. (9+ kg)	3¾–4½ hours

HOMEMADE KITCHEN WREATHS

During the holiday season, I love hanging wreaths everywhere: on the front door, on our wooden garage door, in the living room, and in the kitchen. I make some of the wreaths myself, especially those for the kitchen. I start with a base of pine or fir branches, ivy, or even moss that I've found outside, then I add fresh herbs such as sprigs of sage, rosemary, oregano, and thyme. I hang this wreath over the stove so that I have fresh herbs from the garden at hand when I cook. They dry out over time, of course, but the scent is divine. This makes a nice gift and is a great idea for a workshop with friends over a cup of tea and a slice (or two!) of cake.

POTPOURRI TO FILL YOUR HOME WITH FESTIVE FRAGRANCE

This is a little gift idea that I love! You'll need drawstring bags or small jars, containers, or bowls, as well as twigs or branches and some decorative ribbon, if you wish.

Here are some tried-and-true potpourri combinations:

· Arrange dried orange slices, cinnamon sticks, star anise pods, and pine cones in an attractive container.
· Arrange cinnamon sticks, pine branches, whole cloves, whole nutmeg, fresh cranberries, 1 whole clementine, and 1 star anise pod in an attractive container.
· Combine dried lemon slices, rosemary sprigs, and a cinnamon stick.
· Pour some apple juice into a saucepan and add apple peel, cinnamon sticks, whole cloves, and dried orange slices. Bring to a simmer for a few minutes, then pour into small bowls and place around the house for 3–5 days.

How to make dried citrus slices

Dried citrus slices are pretty and have a wonderful scent—they are also simple to make.

· Preheat the oven to 230°F (110°C/Gas Mark ¼) on fan setting, if available.
· Wash and dry citrus fruit of your choice. Using a very sharp knife, cut the fruit crosswise into approximately ¼-in. (5-mm) slices. Line a baking sheet with parchment paper and place the fruit slices on it in a single layer. Place in the oven for 4 hours, turning the slices over halfway through the cooking time. Transfer them to a rack to finish drying out completely.
· You can use the dried slices to make garlands, to decorate your Christmas tree or table, and to garnish mulled wine or winter cocktails (see Coffee Chai Disco, p. 138).

COFFEE CHAI DISCO

Serves 3–4

ACTIVE TIME
15 minutes, plus preparing
the dried orange slices

INFUSING TIME
2 hours

INGREDIENTS
¾ cup (200 ml) vodka
4 star anise pods, plus extra to decorate
4 chai tea bags (see Kitchen Notes)
⅓ cup (80 ml) coffee liqueur
Scant ½ cup (100 ml) heavy cream
Ice cubes
Ground cinnamon
Cinnamon sticks
Dried orange slices (see p. 134)

1. Pour the vodka into a pitcher, add the star anise pods and tea bags, and let infuse for at least 2 hours.
2. Remove the tea bags and star anise. Mix in the coffee liqueur and heavy cream until combined. Taste and add more vodka, coffee liqueur, or cream, according to your personal taste.
3. Fill cocktail glasses with ice and pour the mixture over. Decorate each cocktail with a small pinch of ground cinnamon, a cinnamon stick, and a dried orange slice.

KITCHEN NOTES: If you cannot find chai tea bags, make your own chai blend by mixing black tea with a little ground cinnamon, ground ginger, ground cloves, freshly grated nutmeg, and ground black pepper. Stir this mixture into the vodka, then strain through a fine-mesh sieve after steeping.

MUSHROOM, SPINACH, AND GOAT CHEESE WREATH

Serves 6

ACTIVE TIME
45 minutes

COOLING TIME
20–25 minutes

COOKING TIME
1¼ hours

INGREDIENTS
1 lb. (500 g) assorted mushrooms
Extra-virgin olive oil
1 yellow onion, finely chopped
1 clove garlic, finely chopped
7 oz. (200 g) baby spinach, chopped
1 tsp cumin seeds
7 oz. (200 g) fresh goat cheese, crumbled
Finely grated zest of 2 lemons, preferably organic
Scant 1 cup (4½ oz./125 g) pine nuts
1 small handful dried cranberries (optional)
2 sheets puff pastry, measuring about 8 × 12 in. (20 × 30 cm), preferably all-butter
3½ tbsp (50 ml) whole milk
Salt and freshly ground pepper

1. Clean and thinly slice the mushrooms. Heat a little olive oil in a skillet, add the onion, garlic, and a pinch of salt, and cook over medium heat until softened. Add the mushrooms and cook until golden.

2. Stir in the spinach and cumin seeds, followed by the goat cheese, lemon zest, pine nuts, and dried cranberries, if using. Season with salt and pepper. Remove from the heat and let cool for 15–20 minutes.

3. Line a baking sheet with parchment paper. Cut one puff pastry sheet in half lengthwise. Place the halves side by side on the baking sheet and cover each one with half the mushroom mixture, leaving a 1½-in. (4-cm) border at each end and a 1¼-in. (3-cm) border along each side.

4. Fold the long sides over the filling to form logs, pressing the pastry edges together to seal. Close the ends, then turn the logs over so the seams are underneath. Very carefully shape the two logs into a wreath. Relax, the difficult part is done!

5. Cut out leaves or flowers from the second pastry sheet. Brush them with a little water and press them gently onto the wreath. This also allows you to hide the joins where the two logs meet.

6. Preheat the oven to 375°F (190°C/Gas Mark 5). Whisk the milk with 1 tbsp olive oil and brush all over the wreath. Bake for 35–40 minutes, until the pastry is puffed and golden brown. Let the wreath cool for several minutes on the baking sheet, then carefully slide it onto a large serving plate.

MINI CHEDDAR, SPINACH, AND CARAMELIZED ONION SCONES

Makes about 20 scones

ACTIVE TIME
20 minutes

COOKING TIME
25 minutes

INGREDIENTS

5 tbsp (2½ oz./70 g) unsalted butter, well chilled, divided

1 large yellow onion, finely chopped

2 cups (9 oz./250 g) all-purpose flour

1 scant tbsp (11 g) baking powder

1 cup (3½ oz./100 g) grated aged Cheddar, divided

1 small handful baby spinach, chopped

1 egg

½ cup (4½ oz./125 g) plain yogurt

1½ tbsp wholegrain mustard

Salt and freshly ground pepper

1. Melt 2 tsp (10 g) butter in a skillet over low heat. Add the onion and a pinch of salt, and cook, stirring occasionally, until the onion is softened and caramelized. Remove from the heat and let cool.

2. In a large bowl, combine the flour and baking powder with a pinch of salt and a pinch of pepper. Dice the remaining butter and work it into the dry ingredients using your fingertips, until the texture is like breadcrumbs.

3. Stir in about ⅔ cup (2½ oz./70 g) of the grated Cheddar, along with the spinach and caramelized onion.

4. In a small bowl, beat together the egg, yogurt, and mustard. Incorporate into the Cheddar mixture until combined.

5. Knead the dough lightly until smooth, adding a little more flour if it is too sticky.

6. Preheat the oven to 400°F (200°C/Gas Mark 6). Line a baking sheet with parchment paper.

7. Roll the dough to a thickness of ¾ in. (2 cm). Cut into about 20 triangles. Place on the baking sheet, sprinkle over the remaining Cheddar, and season with pepper. Bake for 15 minutes, until the scones are golden. Serve warm or at room temperature.

POACHED PEAR AND ROQUEFORT CROSTINI

Makes 18 crostini

ACTIVE TIME
20 minutes

COOLING TIME
15 minutes

COOKING TIME
40 minutes

INGREDIENTS
1¾ cups (450 ml) red wine
Juice of 1 orange
Peel and juice of 1 clementine, preferably
    organic
2 cinnamon sticks
3-4 star anise pods
½ cup (2½ oz./70 g) confectioners' sugar
3 just-ripe, firm pears
6 large slices country bread
About 3½-5½ oz. (100-150 g) Roquefort
Freshly ground pepper
Liquid honey (optional)

1. Warm the red wine, orange juice, clementine peel and juice, cinnamon sticks, star anise, and sugar together in a saucepan over low heat, stirring until the sugar dissolves.
2. Peel the pears and place them whole in the saucepan. Poach them over low heat for about 30 minutes, until they are tender, turning them over from time to time. Remove the pears from the liquid, place on a plate, and let cool.
3. Just before serving, toast the bread slices and cut each one into 3 pieces. Place a little Roquefort on each piece.
4. Halve, core, and slice the pears lengthwise. Place 2-3 slices on each crostini. Season with pepper and, if you wish, drizzle with honey.

FENNEL AND ONION SOUP
WITH COPPA CHIPS

Serves 4–5

ACTIVE TIME
25–30 minutes

COOKING TIME
1 hour

INGREDIENTS
3 tbsp (1½ oz./40 g) unsalted butter
5 yellow onions, finely chopped
1 bulb fennel, finely chopped (reserve
    fronds for garnish)
Juice of 1 orange
2 tbsp apple cider vinegar
1–1½ qt. (1–1.5 L) water
2 sprigs fresh rosemary
5 slices coppa
Salt and freshly ground pepper

1. Melt the butter in a large skillet over low heat. Add the onions, fennel, and a pinch of salt. Cook for about 10 minutes, or until softened.
2. Pour in the orange juice and vinegar and cook for about 15 minutes, stirring occasionally, until the onions and fennel are caramelized.
3. Transfer the onion mixture to a large saucepan or Dutch oven. Pour in 1–1½ qt. (1–1.5 L) water, depending on the consistency desired, and add the rosemary sprigs. Let simmer for 15 minutes.
4. Meanwhile, preheat the oven to 375°F (190°C/Gas Mark 5). Place the coppa on a baking sheet and bake in the oven for 8–10 minutes, until crisp. Let cool on paper towels, then break into small pieces.
5. Remove the rosemary sprigs from the soup. Puree the soup in a blender. Taste and add more salt and pepper, if needed.
6. Transfer the soup to a tureen and top with the coppa chips and chopped fennel fronds. Season with pepper and serve.

RAZOR CLAMS
WITH SPICY HERB BUTTER

Serves 3–4

ACTIVE TIME
15 minutes

SOAKING TIME
1 hour

COOKING TIME
8–10 minutes

INGREDIENTS

2 lb. (1 kg) razor clams

5 tbsp (2½ oz./75 g) butter, diced, at room temperature

¾-in. (2-cm) piece fresh ginger, peeled and grated

2 cloves garlic, finely chopped

Finely grated zest of 1 lemon, preferably organic

2 pinches Cayenne pepper

Leaves of 4 sprigs flat-leaf parsley, chopped and divided

Leaves of 5 sprigs mint, chopped and divided

Fleur de sel

Freshly ground pepper

1. To remove the sand from the clams, soak them in a bowl of salted lukewarm water for 20 minutes. Drain and repeat this process twice more, using fresh water each time.
2. Meanwhile, place the butter, ginger, garlic, lemon zest, and Cayenne pepper in a bowl. Add half the parsley and about two-thirds of the mint, then season with fleur de sel and pepper. Beat together until combined. Chill until needed.
3. Preheat the broiler.
4. Drain the clams and plunge them into boiling salted water for 3 minutes, until their shells open. Drain and discard any that remain closed.
5. Arrange the clams on a rimmed baking sheet and top each one with a little of the flavored butter. Place under the broiler for 3–4 minutes, watching closely to ensure the butter doesn't burn or the clams overcook.
6. Sprinkle with the remaining parsley and mint, and serve immediately.

WINTER SOUP

Serves 5–6

ACTIVE TIME
20–25 minutes

COOKING TIME
40–50 minutes

INGREDIENTS
For the soup
2 carrots
1 leek (white part only)
Extra-virgin olive oil
1 large pinch dried oregano
9 oz. (250 g) chicken breast,
cut into 1¼-in. (3-cm)
pieces

1 yellow onion, finely
chopped
1 garlic clove, finely
chopped
1½ qt. (1.5 L) water
2 bouillon cubes (chicken or
vegetable)
9 oz. (250 g) cooked red
haricot beans
9 oz. (250 g) cooked white
haricot (navy) beans
3 scallions, thinly sliced
9 oz. (250 g) baby spinach
Salt and freshly ground
pepper

For the croutons
3–4 thick slices country
bread
Extra-virgin olive oil
Fleur de sel
Dried herbs and/or spices
of your choice, seeds or
ground (cumin, fennel,
coriander, oregano, etc.)
Generous ¼ cup (1 oz./30 g)
grated Parmesan
Freshly ground pepper

To serve
2–4 tbsp basil pesto (store-
bought or homemade)
Parmesan

1. Peel the carrots and cut them crosswise into ¼-in. (5-mm) slices. Remove any damaged outer layers from the leek, slice in the same way as the carrots, and rinse.
2. Warm a little olive oil in a Dutch oven over medium heat. Add the carrots and leek, season with salt, and stir to coat. Stir in the oregano and let cook for 5 minutes.
3. Add the chicken pieces and onion, stir, and cook for 5–7 minutes, until the chicken is lightly browned. Add the garlic, water, and crumbled bouillon cubes, then bring to a simmer. Simmer gently over low heat for 20–25 minutes.
4. Remove from the heat and stir in the red and white haricot beans, followed by the scallions and spinach. Season with salt and pepper to taste and set aside.
5. To prepare the croutons, preheat the oven to 430°F (220°C/Gas Mark 7). Cut the bread into large cubes. Place them in a bowl, drizzle with olive oil, and toss to coat. Sprinkle with fleur de sel, pepper, your choice of herbs and/or spices, and stir in the Parmesan. Spread over a baking sheet and bake for 10–12 minutes, stirring halfway so they color on all sides, until crisp and evenly golden brown.
6. To serve, reheat the soup, ladle generous servings into soup plates, and add 1–2 teaspoons pesto to each serving. Scatter over the croutons, grate some Parmesan over the top, and serve.

ORANGE AND PISTACHIO SALAD

Serves 4–5

ACTIVE TIME
15–20 minutes

INGREDIENTS
4 blood oranges
2 shallots, thinly sliced
2 tbsp apple cider vinegar
3 tbsp extra-virgin olive oil

1 tsp honey
Fleur de sel
Freshly ground pepper
1–2 oranges
9–10½ oz. (250–300 g)
    mixed lamb's lettuce
    (mâche) and arugula
    (or use baby spinach)
About 10 olives

Leaves of 4–5 sprigs fresh
    cilantro, chopped
Leaves of 4–5 sprigs fresh
    mint, chopped
8 oz. (250 g) burrata, cut into
    pieces
½ cup (2 oz./60 g) shelled
    roasted pistachios,
    chopped
2 pinches sumac (optional)

1. To prepare the dressing, juice 1 blood orange and pour into a bowl. Add the shallots, vinegar, olive oil, and honey, then whisk to combine. Season with fleur de sel and pepper, and set aside.
2. Remove the peel from the regular orange(s) and remaining blood oranges. Cut the fruit crosswise into ⅓-in. (1-cm) slices.
3. To serve, place the lamb's lettuce and arugula (or spinach) on a serving plate. Arrange the orange slices and olives over the top, sprinkle with the herbs, and scatter over the burrata and pistachios. Drizzle over the dressing and sprinkle with sumac, if using. A refreshing, vitamin-rich salad!

ROASTED BRUSSELS SPROUTS WITH CRANBERRIES AND FETA

Serves 4–5, as a side dish

ACTIVE TIME
15 minutes

COOKING TIME
30 minutes

INGREDIENTS
1 lb. (450 g) Brussels sprouts
1–2 cloves garlic, finely chopped
3 tbsp extra-virgin olive oil
1–2 tbsp balsamic vinegar
Fleur de sel
4 oz. (120 g) thick-cut smoked bacon, cut into lardons

1 handful pecan halves, chopped
1 handful dried cranberries
3½ oz. (100 g) feta, crumbled
Fresh chives, snipped, to garnish
Freshly ground pepper

1. Preheat the oven to 400°F (200°C/Gas Mark 6). Line a baking sheet with parchment paper.
2. Wash the Brussels sprouts, cut them in half lengthwise, and spread across the baking sheet. Scatter over the garlic and drizzle with the olive oil and vinegar. Sprinkle with fleur de sel and toss to coat. Bake for 25–30 minutes, until tender and lightly golden, stirring halfway through the cooking time.
3. Meanwhile, cook the bacon lardons in an ungreased skillet over medium-high heat until golden. Drain on paper towels.
4. Place the Brussels sprouts in a serving dish and scatter over the lardons, pecans, cranberries, feta, and snipped chives. Season with pepper and serve immediately.

FENNEL, PEA, AND SAUSAGE STUFFING

Serves 5

ACTIVE TIME
15–20 minutes

COOKING TIME
30 minutes

INGREDIENTS
5–6 thick slices country
  bread
Extra-virgin olive oil
1 tbsp fennel seeds
1 bulb fennel, finely chopped
2 stalks celery, finely
  chopped
2 red onions, finely chopped
Finely grated zest and juice
  of 1 grapefruit, preferably
  organic
3 Toulouse sausages with
  herbs

10½ oz. (300 g) chanterelle
  mushrooms
4 oz. (120 g) frozen peas,
  preferably organic
2 tbsp fresh thyme leaves
2 tbsp chopped fresh sage
  leaves
1½ cups (360 ml) chicken or
  vegetable broth, warm
4–5 slices pancetta, cut into
  pieces
Chopped walnuts (optional)
Salt and freshly ground
  pepper

1. Cut the bread into ½-in. (12-mm) cubes. Heat a little olive oil in a skillet and add the cubed bread, fennel seeds, 2 pinches salt, and pepper. Stir, then fry over medium-high heat until the bread is golden. Drain on paper towels and transfer to a plate.

2. Add a little more olive oil to the same skillet, add the fennel, celery, red onions, and a little salt, and cook until the vegetables have softened. Add the grapefruit juice and remove from the heat.

3. Meanwhile, cut the sausages into ¾–1¼-in. (2–3-cm) slices. Heat a little olive oil in a separate large skillet and fry the sausages with the mushrooms over medium-high heat until browned.

4. Stir in the fennel-celery mixture, followed by the peas, thyme, sage, and, lastly, the bread cubes. Add the broth a little at a time, stirring continuously over medium-high heat. Wait for each addition of stock to be absorbed before adding the next.

5. Add the pancetta to the stuffing, then stir in the grapefruit zest. Taste and add more salt and pepper, if needed.

6. Serve immediately, or make the stuffing ahead and reheat it in a covered dish in a preheated 350°F (180°C/Gas Mark 4) oven. If you wish, sprinkle with chopped walnuts before serving.

STUFFED BUTTERNUT SQUASH

Serves 6–8

ACTIVE TIME
30 minutes

COOKING TIME
1 hour 40 minutes

INGREDIENTS
1 large butternut squash
Extra-virgin olive oil
Fleur de sel
1 yellow onion, finely
  chopped
2 cloves garlic, finely
  chopped
½ cup (3½ oz./100 g) green
  lentils
2 oz. (60 g) dried porcini
  mushrooms
2 pinches ground nutmeg
Leaves of 2 sprigs fresh
  rosemary, finely chopped
Leaves of 3–4 sprigs fresh
  thyme
1 cup (250 ml) vegetable
  broth
3½ oz. (100 g) baby spinach
1 handful chopped roasted
  pistachios
Salt and freshly ground
  pepper

1. Preheat the oven to 350°F (180°C/Gas Mark 4).
2. Cut the butternut squash in half lengthwise and scoop out the seeds. Brush the cut sides with olive oil and sprinkle with fleur de sel. Place cut side up on a baking sheet and bake for 40 minutes, or until the flesh is very tender.
3. Meanwhile, heat a little olive oil in a saucepan over low heat and cook the onion and garlic with a pinch of salt until softened. Add the lentils, porcini mushrooms, nutmeg, rosemary, and thyme, and cook for 2 minutes, stirring continuously. Pour in the broth and simmer over low heat, stirring occasionally, for about 20 minutes, until the lentils are tender. If needed, add a little water during cooking. Stir in the spinach and pistachios, then remove from the heat.
4. Remove the cooked squash from the oven. Carefully scoop out the flesh, leaving a ½-in. (1-cm) layer to avoid piercing the skin and help the squash halves hold their shape. Mash the flesh to a puree, then stir in the lentil mixture.
5. Fill the squash halves with the stuffing. Carefully reshape the squash by placing one half on top of the other. Tie up with kitchen twine at 1¼-in. (3-cm) intervals. Return to the oven for about 10 minutes, until heated through. Cut into thick slices and serve.

KITCHEN NOTES: Serve the squash with a tasty salad.
For a non-vegetarian stuffing, add chopped smoked bacon or a little sausage meat to the pan when frying the onion and garlic.

LEMON ORZO SOUP

Serves 4

ACTIVE TIME
20 minutes

COOKING TIME
20–25 minutes

INGREDIENTS
Extra-virgin olive oil
2 yellow onions, finely
  chopped
Leaves of 4 sprigs fresh sage
9 oz. (250 g) butternut
  squash, diced
2 cloves garlic, finely
  chopped
3 sprigs fresh thyme,
  divided
1½ qt. (1.5 L) chicken
  or vegetable broth
1¼-in. (3-cm) piece fresh
  ginger, peeled
  and grated (optional)
7 oz. (200 g) orzo
Generous 1 cup (9 oz./265 g)
  cooked chickpeas
Juice of 2 lemons
2 oz. (50 g) baby spinach (or
  kale, shredded)
½ lemon, preferably organic
1 pinch fleur de sel
Shaved Parmesan (optional)
Salt and freshly ground
  pepper

1. Heat a little olive oil in a Dutch oven and cook the onions with a pinch of salt over low heat for 3–4 minutes.
2. Chop half the sage leaves and add to the onions, along with the squash, garlic, and the leaves of 2 thyme sprigs. Stir and let cook for 4–5 minutes, then pour in the broth and add the ginger, if using.
3. Bring to a simmer over low heat and cook until the squash is just tender. Stir in the orzo and let cook for 4 minutes, or until it is al dente. Remove from the heat.
4. Stir in the chickpeas, lemon juice, and the spinach (or kale).
5. Cut the lemon half crosswise into ¼-in. (5-mm) slices. Warm a little olive oil and the fleur de sel in a skillet over high heat, add the lemon slices, and sear for 2–3 minutes on each side, until charred in places. Sear the remaining whole sage leaves in the same skillet until crisp. Drain on paper towels.
6. Serve the soup in bowls, topped with the lemon slices and sage leaves. Add a few grinds of pepper, garnish with the remaining thyme sprig broken into small pieces, and sprinkle with shavings of Parmesan, if you wish.

DRIED FRUIT-STUFFED PORK LOIN WITH PEARS

Serves 8–10

ACTIVE TIME
30 minutes

COOKING TIME
About 1 hour 30 minutes

INGREDIENTS
Extra-virgin olive oil
1 yellow onion, finely
   chopped
2 cloves garlic, finely
   chopped

7 oz. (200 g) mixed dried
   fruit, such as apricots,
   figs, and cranberries
Leaves of 3 sprigs fresh
   sage, chopped, plus
   extra to garnish
1 pinch paprika
Scant 1 cup (240 ml) water
Finely grated zest of
   1 orange, preferably
   organic
About 10 cooked
   chestnuts, chopped
1 handful roasted
   hazelnuts, chopped

3½ oz. (100 g) baby spinach
4 lb. (1.8 kg) boneless pork
   loin, butterflied (or ask
   your butcher to do this)
5 tbsp (2¾ oz./75 g)
   unsalted butter
5 small pears
Juice of 1 lemon
1 tbsp maple syrup
Leaves of 1 sprig rosemary,
   chopped, plus extra
   sprigs to garnish
3 tbsp pear jam, warmed
Salt and freshly ground
   pepper

1. Heat a little olive oil in a saucepan and cook the onion and garlic with a pinch of salt over low heat for 4–5 minutes, until softened. Stir in the dried fruit (cutting larger fruit into small pieces), along with the sage and paprika. Let cook for 2 minutes, add the water, and let simmer for 5 minutes. Remove from the heat and let cool. Stir in the orange zest, chestnuts, hazelnuts, and spinach.

2. Open the pork, lay it flat, and season with salt and pepper. Top with the dried fruit mixture, leaving a 1¼ –1½-in. (3–4-cm) border all the way around. Starting at one long side, roll the meat up and tie it at regular intervals using kitchen twine. Preheat the oven to 350°F (180°C/Gas Mark 4).

3. Melt 3 tbsp (1¾ oz./50 g) butter in a Dutch oven over medium heat and brown the pork for 3–4 minutes on all sides. Place in the oven for about 5–10 minutes.

4. Wash the pears, cut them in half lengthwise, and coat with the lemon juice.

5. Melt the remaining butter, mix it with the maple syrup and chopped rosemary, and pour over the pears. Arrange the pears around the pork and cook, uncovered, for 50 minutes. Cover with the lid or aluminum foil and cook for an additional 10 minutes, or until the temperature of the meat reaches 145°F (63°C) in the center.

6. Remove from the oven and brush the roast pork with the warm jam. Cut into 1¼–1½-in. (3–4-cm) slices, garnish with rosemary sprigs and sage leaves, and serve with the pears.

CINNAMON FRENCH TOAST STICKS

Makes about a dozen sticks

ACTIVE TIME
15 minutes

COOKING TIME
20–25 minutes

INGREDIENTS
1 loaf sandwich bread (unsliced)
2 eggs
½ cup (120 ml) whole milk
3–4 tbsp granulated or superfine sugar
1 tsp ground cinnamon
½ tsp ground cardamom
2 pinches fleur de sel
2 tbsp (1 oz./30 g) unsalted butter
Salt

To serve
Maple syrup

1. Cut the bread into 1½–2-in. (4–5-cm) slices. Cut off the crusts, then cut each slice in half into two rectangles.
2. Whisk the eggs in a shallow bowl. Whisk in the milk and a pinch of salt.
3. In a separate shallow bowl, combine the sugar, cinnamon, cardamom, and fleur de sel.
4. Melt the butter in a skillet over medium heat. Quickly dip the bread sticks into the egg mixture to coat all sides, ensuring the ends are coated, too. Place up to 6 sticks at a time in the skillet, depending on its size; the sticks should not be touching. Cook for 2–3 minutes on each side, until golden brown all over.
5. As soon as they are ready, and while they are still hot, dust the sticks with the sugar and spice mixture. Place on a serving plate.
6. Serve warm or at room temperature, with maple syrup on the side for dipping.

HOLIDAY COOKIES

From early December onwards, I love to make a variety of small cookies that I give away to friends, neighbors, my children's teachers, etc.—and, of course, I always keep some at home for teatime or sweet snacks throughout the day. Here are three simple recipes that are always a big hit.

LEMON-THYME SHORTBREADS

Makes 2 dozen cookies
ACTIVE TIME: 15 minutes
CHILLING TIME: 40 minutes
COOKING TIME: 15 minutes per batch
COOLING + SETTING TIME: 20–25 minutes
INGREDIENTS
1¾ sticks (7 oz./200 g) unsalted butter, at room temperature · 1 cup (7 oz./200 g) superfine sugar · 1 egg · 1 tsp vanilla extract · Finely grated zest of 1 lemon, preferably organic · Leaves of 3–4 sprigs fresh thyme · 2¼ cups (10 oz./280 g) all-purpose flour
For the icing
1 egg white · 1 tbsp lemon juice + a little finely grated zest · Confectioners' sugar as needed · Leaves of 3–4 sprigs fresh thyme

Cream together the butter and sugar in a mixing bowl, then beat in the egg and vanilla extract. Stir in the lemon zest and thyme, followed by the flour. Roll the dough between two sheets of parchment paper to a thickness of about ¼ in. (6 mm) and chill for 30 minutes. Meanwhile, preheat the oven to 350°F (180°C/Gas Mark 4). Cut out 1½–2-in. (4–5-cm) disks using a plain cookie cutter and place on two baking sheets lined with parchment paper. Chill for 10 minutes, then bake for 15 minutes, until lightly golden. Let cool. To prepare the icing, whisk together the egg white, lemon juice, and zest in a bowl, then gradually whisk in confectioners' sugar until the icing is the consistency you want (I like mine pretty thick). Spread a little icing on top of each cookie and sprinkle with thyme. Let set for 10–15 minutes.

HOLIDAY BISCOTTI

Makes 15–20 cookies
ACTIVE TIME: 10 minutes
COOKING TIME: 35 minutes
COOLING TIME: 5–6 minutes
INGREDIENTS
Scant ½ cup (3½ oz./100 g) brown sugar · ¼ cup (2 oz./50 g) superfine sugar · 2 tsp vanilla extract · 1 tsp bitter almond extract · 2 eggs · 2 cups (9 oz./250 g) all-purpose flour · 1 tsp baking powder · 2 pinches fleur de sel · Scant 1 cup (3½ oz./100 g) dried cranberries · ¾ cup (3 oz./90 g) shelled pistachios · ⅔ cup (3 oz./90 g) toasted blanched almonds

Preheat the oven to 340°F (170°C/Gas Mark 3). In a mixing bowl, whisk together the brown sugar, superfine sugar, vanilla extract, almond extract, and eggs until combined. Stir in the flour, baking powder, and fleur de sel, then add the cranberries and nuts. Mix well with your hands to make a dough, then shape into two logs about 2¾–3¼ in. (7–8 cm) wide and 7–8 in. (18–20 cm) long. Place on a baking sheet lined with parchment paper and bake for 25–30 minutes, until lightly golden. Remove from the oven, let cool for 5–6 minutes, then cut each log crosswise into 7–10 slices. Place the slices cut side down on the baking sheet, lower the oven temperature to 325°F (160°C/Gas Mark 3), and bake for an additional 8–9 minutes, until dry. Let cool. Feel free to experiment with different spices, dried fruits, or nuts.

PECAN-PISTACHIO BITES

Makes about 30 cookies
ACTIVE TIME: 20 minutes
COOKING TIME: 10–12 minutes
COOLING TIME: 8–10 minutes
INGREDIENTS
2 sticks (7¾ oz./220 g) unsalted butter, diced and softened · ⅔ cup (3 oz./80 g) confectioners' sugar, plus extra for dusting · A few drops of vanilla extract · 2 pinches fleur de sel · 2½ cups (10½ oz./300 g) all-purpose flour · Generous ½ cup (2½ oz./70 g) pecan halves · Generous ½ cup (2½ oz./70 g) shelled pistachios

Preheat the oven to 350°F (180°C/Gas Mark 4). Place the butter, sugar, vanilla extract, and fleur de sel in a large bowl, and beat until combined. Stir in the flour. Grind the pecans and pistachios to a powder, leaving a few larger pieces, and mix into the dough. Roll into balls slightly smaller than golf balls and place on a baking sheet lined with parchment paper. Bake for 10–12 minutes, until lightly golden. Let cool for about 10 minutes, so the cookies firm up and don't crumble when removed from the sheet. Place a little confectioners' sugar in a soup plate and roll the cookies in it until well coated.

HOMEMADE FORTUNE COOKIES

Makes about 20 cookies

ACTIVE TIME
15 minutes

COOKING TIME
7 minutes per batch

INGREDIENTS
1 stick (4 oz./115 g) unsalted butter
3 egg whites
¾ cup (5 oz./150 g) superfine sugar
½ tsp bitter almond extract
1 tbsp orange flower water
2 tbsp water
1 cup (4 oz./120 g) all-purpose flour

For the messages
About 20 slips of paper measuring
    approximately 3 × ½ in. (8 × 1 cm) with
    a sweet message written on them

1. Preheat the oven to 375°F (190°C/Gas Mark 5). Line a baking sheet with parchment paper. Have a muffin pan or some small glasses handy for cooling the shaped cookies when they come out of the oven.
2. Heat the butter gently in a saucepan until just melted, then set aside. In a mixing bowl, whisk together the egg whites and sugar for 2–3 minutes until they hold soft peaks. Slowly whisk in the melted butter, then whisk in the almond extract, orange flower water, and water. Fold in the flour, taking care not to overwork the batter.
3. Place a tablespoon of batter on the baking sheet and spread it into a circle measuring approximately 3 in. (7–8 cm) in diameter. Repeat 4 or 5 times: I recommend baking a maximum of 4–5 cookies at a time so they can be folded while still hot and soft.
4. Bake for 7 minutes, until the edges are lightly golden. As each batch comes out of the oven, let cool for 30 seconds, then quickly shape each cookie: remove using a spatula, place in the palm of your hand (the side facing up in the oven should face down in your hand), then fold in half, tucking one of your messages in between the top and bottom halves. Place the folded side of the semicircle over the rim of a glass or bowl and gently fold the ends down to make a fortune cookie shape.
5. Place each cookie in the cavity of a muffin pan or in a small glass so that it holds its shape as it cools. Most importantly, don't worry—you'll quickly get the hang of it!

KITCHEN NOTES: I love asking my sons to help write the messages and decorate the slips of paper with colorful drawings.

LIST OF RECIPES